Love, Marriage—and Jesus

Love, Marriage—and Jesus

The Song of Solomon

JONATHAN F. BAYES

RESOURCE *Publications* · Eugene, Oregon

LOVE, MARRIAGE—AND JESUS
The Song of Solomon

Resource Publications
An Imprint of Wipf and Stock Publishers
199 W. 8th Ave., Suite 3
Eugene, OR 97401

www.wipfandstock.com

PAPERBACK ISBN: 978-1-6667-3242-9
HARDCOVER ISBN: 978-1-6667-2611-4
EBOOK ISBN: 978-1-6667-2612-1

09/29/21

I dedicate this work to my wife Cathy, a model wife, who sacrificed the opportunities to gain qualifications or pursue a career in order to care for a husband, a family, and a home—truly a godly example.

Contents

Contents

1

The Most Excellent Song

(Song of Solomon 1:1)[1]

The Song of Solomon is a joyful and beautiful affirmation of love in the context of marriage. Marriage is one of God's most special gifts to the human race. Living as we do at a time when marriage is despised and corrupted, this part of God's inspired word is an invitation from the Creator to join him in celebrating this wonderful gift of human love.

The first verse reads:

> The song of songs, which *is* Solomon's.[2]

1. This is a revised edition of my earlier book, *Sex, Love, and Marriage—a Celebration: The Song of Solomon*. I now think that in that previous edition I played down too much the illustrative aspect of the Song as symbolic of the love between Christ and his people, and exaggerated certain aspects of married love. While I still endorse the wisdom of God for married life which is offered to us in this inspired writing, and while I still reject the purely allegorical reading of the Song, I now seek to redress the balance, recognizing that the marriage described in the Song is a pointer to the highest love of all—that between the Lord Jesus Christ and his people, his bride, the church. I trust that this will make the work more relevant to Christians in general, rather than primarily aiming at counsel for married couples.

2. Scripture quotations (unless otherwise indicated) are from the New

This is simply the title. It identifies the human author, Solomon, who composed this song under the inspiration of the Holy Spirit; and it amounts to the claim to be the most excellent of all songs, a description which has been eloquently expanded upon in these words:

> "The Song of songs" means the most excellent song, the outstanding song, the pre-eminent song. It carries the sense of the all-surpassing song, the most highly treasured and praiseworthy song, the unrivalled song. There is no song like it, none to compare with it, either among divinely inspired songs or songs of merely human composition. No other song comes near it. It stands alone.[3]

And little wonder that this is the most excellent of songs, because it is on the most excellent of all themes—as Paul makes clear when he refers in 1 Corinthians 12:31 to the "more excellent way," which he then proceeds, in chapter 13, to define as the way of love. It is a valid observation regarding The Song of songs that "it is difficult to find its equal as a piece of writing on human love."[4]

However, the Song of Solomon is a difficult book. Some of its wording can even seem a bit embarrassing to devout readers. Maybe it is for that reason that it has often been read as pure allegory. The claim then is that the Song of Solomon is not really about human love at all. That seems to be the surface meaning, but it is totally irrelevant. The real meaning, so the argument goes, is hidden. The Song of Solomon is actually about, and is only about, the love between God and his people (on a Jewish reading), or between Christ and believers (which is the Christian interpretation). Allegory totally ignores any earthly reference and leaps straight into an exposition of that higher love. That way of understanding the book has been true in Christian interpretation, but also by many Jewish interpreters.

Let me just mention one example each of a Christian and a Jewish reading of the book along those lines. The seventeenth-century

---

King James Version.

3. Brooks, *Song*, 13.

4. Balchin, *Song*, 579.

Scottish preacher, James Durham, writes: "The divine mystery intended and set forth here is the mutual love and spiritual union, and communion that is betwixt Christ and his church."[5] And, from a Jewish background, the eleventh-century rabbi and commentator, Shlomo Yitzhaki, commonly known simply as Rashi, says this: "Our rabbis taught: Every Solomon . . . mentioned in the Song of Songs is sacred (it refers to God), the King to whom peace belongs."[6]

However, there is a real problem with such an approach, because if we assume that the Song is nothing but an allegorical account of the relationship between Jesus and his church, the danger is that anyone can find any hidden meaning that they want to. There are no controls on what we find in the book. If we disregard the obvious meaning, then who knows where we might end up, and what fancy ideas we might invent?

Professor John Murray was a minister of the Free Church of Scotland who went over to the States to teach at Westminster Theological Seminary. In 1983 a passage from a letter which he had written about the Song of Solomon was quoted in the Free Church magazine. This is what he said:

> I cannot now endorse the allegorical interpretation of the Song of Solomon. I think the vagaries of interpretation given in terms of the allegorical principle indicate that there are no well-defined hermeneutical canons to guide us in determining the precise meaning and application if we adopt the allegorical view.[7]

To put that more simply, what Professor Murray is saying is this. When you have to find a hidden meaning in the Song of Solomon, when you argue that what the book seems to be saying it is not saying at all, you end up with a huge variety of interpretations, some of which may be rather comical. This simply proves that no rules exist for finding out what the Song really means if you treat it as an allegory. You can make it mean anything you want to. You are

5. Durham, *Exposition*, 32.
6. Rashi, *Commentary*, on Song of Sol. 1:1.
7. Free Church of Scotland, "John Murray," 52.

then on dangerous ground. There is no way of knowing whether you have wandered into serious error.

So it is much better to start by taking the Song of Solomon at face value. It is, before all else, a celebration of the love between a man and a woman as God the Creator intended it to be within the context of marriage. It is an invitation to rejoice with God in the pleasure which he has built into human life and relationships.

Having said that, of course, in one sense it must be right that the book has got to be about the love between Christ and his church. After all, in Luke 24:27 we read this about what Jesus said to the pair on the road to Emmaus: "And beginning at Moses and all the Prophets, he expounded to them in all the Scriptures the things concerning himself." The words "all the Scriptures" must include this book.

And we do know that human love in the bond of marriage is intended by God as a visual aid to help us understand something of the love between Christ and the church. In Ephesians 5:22–33 the apostle talks about the relationship between husband and wife, but in verse 32 he writes, "This is a great mystery, but I speak concerning Christ and the church." Throughout that passage teaching about human marriage and teaching about the relationship between Christ and the church are intricately interwoven. And that is not surprising, because human love is patterned on the love that Christ has for the church. So when you look at a marriage, particularly a Christian marriage, which is functioning well, you can see a beautiful picture of how Christ and his church are in love with each other.

So it would certainly be quite wrong to say that the Song of Solomon has nothing to do with the love of God for his people or of Christ for believers. Indeed, the very fact that the Song is a celebration of human loving drives us on to hear in its singing the new song of joyful union between the Lord Jesus Christ and his beloved bride, the church.

And, actually, John Murray would agree. Having rejected the allegorical interpretation of the Song, the quotation which I gave above continues like this:

However, I also think that in terms of biblical analogy the Song could be used to *illustrate* the relation of Christ to his church. The marriage bond is used in Scripture as a pattern of Christ and the church. If the Song portrays marital love and relationship on the highest levels of exercise and devotion, then surely it may be used to exemplify what is transcendently true in the bond that exists between Christ and the church.[8]

This seems to me a more promising way of reading the Song. It means that the picture painted on the earthly level is an illustration, a symbol, of the higher relationship between Christ and his people. The advantage of this approach is that we have to start by understanding the human message before applying it to Christ and the church. Indeed, you cannot truly hear that love song between Christ and his people, unless you have first listened properly to Solomon's love song on the purely human plane. From there we are led upwards to a higher level where we can appreciate something of heavenly love.

This prevents our imagination from running away with itself. We no longer feel free, as we might do if we treat the book as an allegory, to ignore the human scene, and come up with whatever interpretations take our fancy, whether or not they genuinely arise from the text. To hear the human love song as an illustration of the relationship between Christ and his people exerts a discipline on us. We have first to work hard to understand, as best we can, what is going on at the earthly level, and only then make the application to the love between Christ and his bride. The application is then restricted and controlled by what is actually happening in the human drama.[9]

That does not mean that the love described on the human level is just a slightly embarrassing necessity to get us up on to that higher plane. The human love story is not an unfortunate hurdle that we have to get over in order to hear the music of that "love divine, all loves excelling."

8. Free Church of Scotland, "John Murray," 52.

9. Stuart Olyott takes a similar approach, classifying it as 'typical,' in contrast with the allegorical approach, which he, too rejects (*Life Worth Living*, 76–79).

Rather, the truth is that the Song of Solomon works both ways. The human love song does indeed point to that greatest love in all eternity, that love which Galatians 2:20 celebrates, "the Son of God, who loved me and gave himself for me." But then the very fact that the Bible paints this picture of divine love in terms of the love between a man and his wife sends us back down to earth again. We recognize that there is absolutely nothing to be embarrassed about in the story of the relationship between a man and a woman in that proper context of marriage. Rather, it is something to be celebrated, something to rejoice in, something to enter into with passion and pleasure. So as we read the Song of Solomon, the human love story points us upwards to God's love. And then, thinking about that, we are brought down to earth again to celebrate human love, and, indeed, to respond to the challenge to ensure that our human marriages really are genuine reflections of that greatest of all loves.

So now we need to ask this question: who are the man and his wife in the Song of Solomon? Quite a few different answers have been given,[10] but it seems to me fairly obvious that the happy couple are Solomon himself and his wife, probably Pharaoh's daughter. We learn from 1 Kings 3:1 that she was Solomon's first wife. In addition to the opening verse, Solomon is referred to another six times in the book (in 1:5 we hear of "the curtains of Solomon," in 3:7 of "Solomon's couch," 3:9 and 11 refer to "Solomon the King" and "King Solomon," and 8:11 and 12 describe Solomon's vineyard). So Solomon seems to be one of the main characters.

In chapter 6 and verse 13 the woman is twice called "Shulamite," and this is the only verse where this word appears in the whole Bible. There are several different interpretations of this name, but the one that commends itself to me informs us that "Shulamite" is simply the feminine form of "Solomon."[11] If that is so, then, in

10. The position advocated by, for example, William Still, which paints Solomon as a villain, and sees the girl's true lover as a peasant shepherd (*Song*, 7–9), seems to me to have little to commend it; Martin, rightly in my view, finds the objections to this theory to be "fatal" ("Proverbs, Ecclesiastes, Song of Songs," 295).

11. Goodspeed, *Shulammite*, 103.

modern talk, "Shulamite" could be translated "Mrs. Solomon." I suspect that this is what it means.

And it is the relationship between Solomon and his wife, Shulamite, Mrs. Solomon, which is being used as an example of married love, to which every couple may aspire. What we have here is a love song which is sung between Solomon and his wife.

From what we know of Solomon's love life the picture which he paints in this song is clearly rather idealized. 1 Kings 11:1 says, "But King Solomon loved many foreign women as well as the daughter of Pharaoh." It goes on to describe how all these foreign women turned his heart away from the Lord.

I imagine that Solomon wrote the Song late in life when he had an opportunity to look back on the way that he had lived. It caused him great regret. Now he wants to teach others to avoid his mistakes. In reality, I suspect, Solomon missed out on the potential joy of a deeply loving marriage, because he had taken all these other women as well. But now, in composing this song towards the end of his life, he admits, wistfully, what might have been. If only! He is inspired to describe what God intended, as if to say to us all: aim at this; do not do what I did. Then your life will be a permanent celebration of joy.

As a song, this book of Scripture is a work of the imagination. It is poetic. It is a work of art. The late nineteenth-century artist, Claude Monet, represented the school of art known as "Impressionism." According to Impressionism (and, admittedly, I am over-simplifying things a bit) a work of art is designed to convey a general impression, and not to be specific at every single point. Impressionistic painters had an influence on certain musicians. Monet's younger contemporary, Claude Debussy, introduced impressionism to music.

I like to think of the Song of Solomon as something of an impressionistic song. It is intended to convey an impression. As a love song, the impression it wants to convey is that it is worth celebrating the love of a man and a woman within marriage.

But just because the Song is impressionistic, interpretation is tricky. Two people can look at a work of art and think that it is about entirely different things. And when you read the commentaries on the Song of Solomon, you find that there are many different inter-pretations of various verses and passages. That suggests to me that we would be unwise to try to squeeze some meaning out of every little detail. If we try to press for some significance in every word or every line, we lose something of what the Song is really all about. It is written in picture language. To over-explain it is to risk squeez-ing all meaning out of it. There are some lines in the Song, in fact, which are quite impossible to understand. None of the commenta-tors tell us what they mean, because everyone is baffled.

But the general impression—the wonderful blessing of a God-given relationship of love between a man and a woman within the context of marriage—that comes over clearly enough. So that is what we must take from the Song—the general impression. Its pur-pose is to commend to every married couple what they may enjoy by the goodness of God.

And, of course, we must not forget that the marriage relation-ship between man and wife points beyond itself to God's love in Christ for his people. And when we have looked up through this description of human marriage to that love, then we are brought back down to earth again with a new determination, in the light of God's love, to enjoy love in marriage for God's sake.

The nineteenth-century composer Franz Schubert wrote some Song Cycles. A Song Cycle is a series of songs around a common theme. There is an artistic unity to the cycle, though each song is distinct and has its own miniature theme within the big theme.

The Song of Solomon is a bit like a Song Cycle. It is a series of episodes, looking at this wonderful gift of love in marriage from various angles. Different aspects are presented. The Song is not tracing the development of marriage through life. It does not start with the wedding and go through "until death us do part." When the Song begins Solomon and Shulamite are an established married couple. But quite soon there is a flashback to the days before they were married. Then later on in the Song we have a passage which is clearly a reference to the wedding, but it comes in the middle, not at the beginning. Solomon is not interested in chronology. The point is simply to bring out various aspects of the happiness of the state of marriage. Some aspects are brought out through the experience of a couple who have been married for years. Other aspects are highlighted by contrasting marriage with the days of courtship. Others again emerge through the excitement of newly-weds, and so on. The author wants to convey an impression, and so to invite us to join him in rejoicing in the good gift that God has given, in celebrating married love.

All that we have said so far means that we have to say a word about the relevance of this book for single people. Is there anything here for you if you have not been married? Well, first of all, you are maybe hoping that one day you will find your lifelong soulmate and enjoy your wedding day and the married life that follows. The Song of Solomon may serve to whet your appetite; it may provide lessons in advance which will put you in good stead when your happy day comes.

But of course there are some people for whom marriage is not part of God's purpose. And the Song of Solomon must certainly not be read as implying that a single life is a substandard life or a miserable existence. We know from Paul's words in 1 Corinthians 7 that there is huge potential, there are great possibilities, in being single, there are opportunities which are denied to married couples. This is what the apostle says there in verses 32 and 33:

> He who is unmarried cares for the things of the Lord—
> how he may please the Lord. But he who is married cares
> about the things of the world—how he may please his
> wife.

And if you are called to lifelong singleness, the Song of Solomon may still help you to praise God for the blessings which have come to you because of God's gift to the human race of marriage— the love of your parents for example, or the love of a couple who have befriended you and welcomed you into their home and their hearts. I remember how, in my earliest days away from home as a student, a lovely couple, Sunday after Sunday, would invite me back for lunch and tea after the morning service, and I was embraced within their love.

But supremely, of course, all of us, whether we are single or married, may hear in the Song of Solomon the joyful celebration of the greatest love of all—what Paul in Ephesians 3:19 calls "the love of Christ which passes knowledge." All of us who belong to the Lord Jesus Christ, whether we are single or married, may anticipate through this Song that glorious coming day when we shall hear the summons of Revelation 19:7: "Let us be glad and rejoice and give him glory, for the marriage of the Lamb has come, and his wife has made herself ready." That day is described in Revelation 21:2, where John foresaw "the holy city, New Jerusalem [meaning the entire church redeemed in Christ], coming down out of heaven from God, prepared as a bride adorned for her husband."

And so, whatever our state on earth, we can look forward to heaven when all God's people shall be married—to Christ himself forever, in the bliss of a relationship to which the very best human marriage is just a very faint pointer.

2

Joy and Demand

(Song of Solomon 1:2–6)

In a sense, this impressionistic song cycle, the Song of Solomon, is a work of fiction. Solomon is pondering, probably towards the end of his life, what an ideal marriage would be like. He's thinking about what his marriage to his wife, Shulamite, could have been. But his marriage was not like this at all. So it would be quite wrong to try to find in every detail in the Song a reference to something that actually happened. Solomon is being led by the Holy Spirit to give us an impression: we are impressed by the fact that marriage is a wonderful gift for which we should be seriously and joyfully thankful. So Solomon's God-given purpose in writing is, first of all, to commend to every married couple what they may enjoy by God's goodness.

But, as mentioned in the previous chapter, there is also a higher purpose in the book. It points us upwards to the greatest love of all—that between the Lord Jesus Christ and his bride, the church.

So our question right now has to be: what impression of love within marriage is conveyed by Song of Solomon 1:2–6?

But just before we embark on our study, I need to make another introductory comment. One thing that is difficult in interpreting the Song is to know at some points who is speaking and to whom. It is obvious enough in certain parts of the Song, but there are passages where it is not immediately obvious. So in many Bibles the translators or editors have tried to help us. They have added headings which allocate some verses to Shulamite (the wife), others to the Beloved (the husband), and others to further participants in the drama, such as the daughters of Jerusalem, Shulamite's brothers, and the Beloved's friends, and sometimes they also try to clarify who is being addressed at any particular point.

But we have to remember that those headings are not inspired. They are not present in the original text. They have been added to help us to make sense of the book. But the problem is that not everyone agrees on exactly how the verses should be allocated, so in the end some of them are just guesses, and you will find differences between different Bibles. This means that the headings can be misleading. I have found that sometimes I have come to a different conclusion from the editors of the New King James Version. And here I think the publishers of the Authorized Version were much wiser, in that they did not insert these non-inspired lines. So in our study the headings present in the New King James Version will be ignored, and I shall indicate as we proceed how I think that the words that we are considering should be allocated.

What impression of love within marriage, then, do we gain from the present passage? Two themes seem to emerge.

THE MAGNIFICENT JOY OF MARRIED LOVE (VERSES 2-4).

As the Song gets underway after the title of verse 1, we hear, I think, the wife speaking. And in the first line of verse 2 she is speaking to herself—she is musing. She is longing to receive her husband's expression of love: the very first thing she says is that she wants him to kiss her. She is expressing to herself her desire for her husband.

But then, apparently, her longed-for husband suddenly bursts upon the scene. He has probably been out and about fulfilling the duties of the day, and now he has arrived home. And in the second part of verse 2 Shulamite starts speaking to her husband directly, and she continues speaking until the middle of verse 4, when, very briefly, we hear his voice, and then she resumes her expression of longing love.

First of all, she gladly tells her husband: "your love is better than wine." The Hebrew word translated "love" here is a fairly unusual one. It is derived from a root which means "to boil." So it denotes the hot passion for each other felt by a couple who are in love. And as far as the wife is concerned, her husband's love is something that she enjoys far more than the best vintage wine.

And as she continues in verse 3, she is still expressing the delight of being with her husband. She compares his very name to "good ointments" (or it could be fragrant oils), which have been "poured forth" to release their sweet scent. And these references to wine in verse 2 and now ointments in verse 3 combine to express the sheer pleasure of love, the pure joy of this highest of all human relationships. Both of these things—wine and ointment—are used in the Bible as emblems of gladness and delight. For example, Psalm 104:15 speaks of "wine that makes glad the heart of man," and Proverbs 27:9 says that "ointment and perfume delight the heart." So in speaking of these two things here, the woman is simply saying to her husband, there is nothing that brings me greater pleasure than your love.

In verse 4 she is excitedly inviting her husband to exert his magnetic pull upon her heart, to draw her away from lesser concerns into the intimacy of love. And when he beckons her to come, there will be no hesitation on her part: she will come—and come running at that. And immediately she finds herself in his chambers, in the secret place, where there are just him and her to enjoy one another without interruption or intrusion from outside their happy relationship.

Although the word "chambers" is used mostly in the Old Testament to refer to a literal room in a house or a tent, there are two verses in Proverbs 20, verses 27 and 30, which speak of "the inner depths [literally, the chambers] of the heart." And as Shulamite withdraws with Solomon into the seclusion of the secret place, she feels that he has genuinely taken her into his heart—and that is what gives her such a thrill and so much joy.

In the fourth line of verse 4 we hear the husband speak for the first time. He says, in poetic language, "we will be glad and rejoice in you." Like his wife, he too knows that, as they share each other's love, in being together, the two of them unitedly experience the joy that they find in each other. Love is a bond of true and deep union.

And then the wife chips in again, affirming that the magnificent joy of married love is a pleasure that is better than a glass of wine.

If you have got a copy of the New King James Version to hand, you will notice a difference in this passage between my reading and the view of the editors of the translation. I have come to the conclusion that, apart from four places, there are only two characters who speak (or should we say, sing) in this Song, Shulamite and Solomon. So I am not persuaded that the daughters of Jerusalem, who are mentioned by Shulamite in verse 5, are actually the speakers in the second, and the fourth and fifth lines of verse 4. I read those lines as Shulamite and Solomon rejoicing together in what "we"—the two of them, may enjoy in their marital union. If you like, as each of them speaks in turn, it is akin to a royal "we": they thereby express their sense of immense privilege at being together in marital intimacy. This means that the unknown author of this anonymous chorus captured the sentiment exactly:

> I will rejoice in you and be glad,
> I will extol your love more than wine,
> Draw me after you and let us run together,
> I will rejoice in you and be glad.

So the main point of these verses is the magnificent joy of it all. And God has given us marriage to bring us joy, a joy so magnificent that it is better than any other happiness that is possible on earth. So we are invited to celebrate that fact, to rejoice in God's gift.

But perhaps there is a bit of a challenge in these words as well. When we hear Shulamite talking as she does here, it makes us check that there is nothing defective in our marriages. Maybe we husbands need to hear this challenge. Do our wives feel like this? Each of us needs to ask ourself, does my wife think that there is nothing better in all the world, nothing calculated to make her happier, than my love for her? Or is there something lacking in the husband's love for his wife?

Interestingly, in the Song of Solomon, the challenges to husbands seem to be stronger than the challenges to wives.[1] Maybe that is quite intentional. Solomon writes as a man who failed in marriage. Perhaps he intends the Song to be a message to men. In Ephesians 5:22–33, similarly, the apostle has a lot more to say to husbands than to wives. After three verses exhorting wives, he then takes nine verses to press upon husbands their duty of Christlike love for their wives. Maybe that is because we men have to work at these things more than the women do, in order to reach the ideal marriage that is portrayed by the Song.

But that reference to Christlike love calls us to lift our sights higher. We remember that the bride of Christ, the church, knows the joy of his love. Just as Shulamite longs for Solomon, so the church longs for Jesus Christ, and enjoys him above everything else. We long for the day of his appearing when the celestial wedding day will take place. But even now, I trust that every day we long for a closer walk with Jesus, a deeper affection for Jesus in our hearts, a more powerful sense of the nearness to us of our Savior. Compared with the best things in this world—wine and ointment, or whatever the equivalents may be in our day or in our personal preferences—the love of the Lord is far more exalted. It puts the happiest of earthly pleasures deeply in the shade.

It is a wonderful thought that Jesus has us in the chambers of his heart. He says to us that one line which Solomon speaks here to his wife; "we will be glad and rejoice in you." Is that not a staggering thought that our Savior finds gladness and joy in us! You would not think that he needed us. He has known the joy of heaven since all eternity. He has experienced the gladness of his Father's love since before time began. And yet his most magnificent joy is found in his relationship with the people whom he has taken to his heart. And, together with him, we too rejoice in the reality of his love.

There is another challenge, isn't there? We need to pray constantly for a closer intimacy with Jesus in our daily experience. We

---

1. Far more lines are attributable to Shulamite than to Solomon—a fact which leads Carr to comment, "This is really *her* book" (*Song*, 130).

need to enter his chamber, wherever that may be, and spend time alone with him in the seclusion of the secret place of prayer, in fellowship with him as we listen to him speaking in his word every single day. Yes, there truly is magnificent joy in knowing the love of Jesus, the love that he demonstrated in his death for us as sinners, and when we come to him as sinners, in need of forgiveness, depending on his death to save us, we find that we really have embarked on a life of magnificent joy.

Now just a by-the-way: I have not so far commented on the last line of verse 3 and the last line of verse 4. Who are these virgins who love Shulamite's husband? I do not think that they are anybody in particular. The wife is simply reveling in the fact that she has a husband who is widely respected by others. It is in that sense that she uses the word "love" here, I think. She is saying, other people admire you, and that makes me happy.

So if we husbands want our wives to be able to revel in the fact that we are appreciated and admired by other people, we had better make sure that we live in such a way that other people do respect us!

But of course, for the believer, nothing makes us happier than seeing our beloved Lord Jesus being adored by other people, especially those who have never adored him before. The joy which he feels as sinners are saved is one which he shares with us, and so we celebrate when we hear news of conversions, do we not?

So the first of our two themes from this passage was the magnificent joy of married love, and now, we notice the second theme:

THE DEMANDING RESPONSIBILITY
OF MARRIED LOVE (VERSES 5–6).

In these verses the wife continues speaking, but this time she is addressing "the daughters of Jerusalem." In the commentaries you will find umpteen different suggestions as to who they might be. In my opinion they represent young women in general. Shulamite speaks to them several times in the course of the Song. Their presence serves both to add vividness and color to the song, but also to provide the opportunity for some important teaching on the theme of love and marriage. At this early point in the Song we are to understand that the couple have been married for some years.

The sense of lines 1, 3, and 4 of verse 5 can best be brought out by putting it like this: "I am dark, but lovely, dark like the tents of Kedar, yet lovely like the curtains of Solomon." So a contrast is being depicted between darkness and loveliness, which is illustrated by reference to the difference between the tents and the curtains.

So Shulamite admits that she is dark like those Kedar tents. Apparently, the people of Kedar used to make their tents with the skins of black goats. The reason why the wife is that dark is that she has a sun tan, as verse 6 indicates. Today, I get the impression that most young women would give anything to have a sun tan, or at least a tan, even if it is obtained by an artificial tanning method. But as far as Shulamite was concerned it was not something to be proud of. In those days people got a sun tan if they were not of sufficient social standing to be able to stay indoors out of the sun. They were from the lower orders of society, and had to do outdoor work, but outdoor work was burdensome.

But here we are dealing in picture language. Shulamite is pointing out that there is something burdensome about marriage, in particular, at this point, for the woman. There are responsibilities to shoulder. There are demands which take their toll. Perhaps to people in general, especially to the younger generation, she looks merely dark, unattractive.

But then she says, I am "lovely." To her husband she is lovely indeed, as lovely as "the curtains of Solomon." After we moved into a new house we had to buy some new curtains. We selected them from the range at a supplier, fairly local to where we now live. But that supplier's curtains, even their loveliest productions, are nothing compared with the curtains of Solomon. When Solomon built the temple he hung there the veil, the curtain "of blue, purple, crimson, and fine linen" (2 Chronicles 3:14). Shulamite says, yes, the burdensome responsibility of marriage has taken its toll on me, and that's what young women notice, they think I'm past it, but as far as my husband's concerned, I'm as lovely as the finest curtains.

In the last three lines of verse 6, I think that the first two lines are really just preparing the way for the third. We do not need to inquire too closely what they mean. Shulamite's main point is stated in the last line: "my own vineyard I have not kept." What that means is "I am married." The vineyard is used several times in the Song as a symbol of femininity. She is saying, I've presented that to my husband; I haven't kept it; I'm married; that's made me dark; it's taken its toll on me, but to my husband I'm lovely; the responsibilities of married life have had their effect on me, but still my husband admires me.

Every husband needs to remember as he grows older that so does his wife. It may be, as the years go by, that all that other people notice are the wrinkles, the greying hair, the stooped shoulders—the darkness. But with the husband it is different. He sees in those very features his wife's loveliness. They are the marks of a life of demanding responsibility in being married to him. She has fulfilled those responsibilities so faithfully, so cheerfully, so selflessly, with so little grumbling. At times the wife has had to battle through her own emotions to wait on her husband, when he was scarcely aware of her struggles. And the very darkness is the loveliness as far as the husband is concerned.

A husband needs always to keep his wife's loveliness before his eyes. She has not kept herself for herself. She has allowed him to possess her. What a sacrifice! What a demanding responsibility!

Well now, a husband might feel like protesting, but I have burdens and responsibilities too. Well, that may be so, but it is not what these verses are talking about, so that is not our theme just now. As husbands, we need to overcome our selfishness, forget about our own burdens, and thank our wives for their loveliness. After all, isn't it usually the case that the burdens and responsibilities of marriage are harder on the wife than on the husband? So as far as the husband is concerned, he needs to remember that her loveliness grows by the month—and he needs to tell her, and thank her.

And I guess, as we lift our gaze to the heavenly realm, we are aware that the stresses and strains of the Christian life do take their toll. When we were newly converted, perhaps we were bursting with enthusiasm. Now, as the years, for some of us, the decades, have passed, we know only too well that the Christian life, for all its magnificent joy, is also a life of demanding responsibility. As one old hymn puts it:

> There's a fight to be fought,
> And a race to be run,
> There are dangers to meet by the way.[2]

And we can feel worn down, tired out, and yet deep down we still want to keep on giving our all for Jesus. And the wonderful thing is, that like the ideal husband in the Song of Solomon, he is fully appreciative of every burden which we have borne in our service for him, our life with him. He knows every trial we have faced, every risk we have taken, every demanding responsibility which we have shouldered in his name. We claim no credit, of course, but our hearts are uplifted by the realization that he looks at us today, far more wrinkled than we were twenty years ago, far more grey-haired than we were in our youth, far less energetic than we used to be, and he loves us not one bit less than he did when we first became Christians, than he did in those days when our enthusiasm ran wild for him.

And today, as weakness starts to overtake us, as we have struggled with uncertainties that we would never have dreamed would afflict us years back, as we have battled against temptations which earlier on we thought we would have mastered decades ago, but no, it was not quite like that—for all that, the Savior gazes upon us with wide opened eyes and says to you and to me, you are so lovely.

Sometimes, if we buy curtains from an internet supplier, we might find when we get them that the color is not exactly as it looked in the pictures in the online catalog. We might mull things over for a day or two. Will they do, or shall we send them back and get a refund? Well, I can assure you: there is no danger whatsoever that the Lord will ever mull things over like that: shall I keep this one, or send him back, send her back, to where he/she came from? No, we are loved with an everlasting love, loved from eternity, loved to an endless eternity, as loved by Jesus today, as lovely to Jesus today, as when our names were first recorded in the Lamb's Book of Life. Hallelujah!

2. Author unknown.

3

Secure Togetherness

(Song of Solomon 1:7–8)

In the opening section of the Song of Solomon we heard Shulamite speaking as a married woman about the magnificent joys and the demanding responsibilities of married love which she and Solomon had experienced over the years that they had spent together as husband and wife.

The next two verses are a flashback to the days before Solomon and Shulamite were married. As we have already mentioned, Solomon's intention in this Song is not to write a chronological account of the development of love from courtship to the wedding and on into married life. He wants to convey an impression. His mission is to remind and convince us that the married life is a life worth celebrating as the pinnacle of God's gifts to the human race. And he does so by jumping backwards and forwards, writing a cycle of miniature songs, each of which makes its own contribution to that all-encompassing impression.

The next pair of verses, then, takes us back to the days when Solomon and Shulamite were a courting couple. Their message is the secure togetherness of married love.

These verses form a conversation. In verse 7 the woman speaks and in verse 8 the man replies. We can infer that these verses are a flashback because of the word used in the first line of verse 7. The woman addresses the man as "you whom I love," and the word "love" translates the same Hebrew verb as that used at the end of verses 3 and 4. There Shulamite refers to the love of the virgins for Solomon. In the previous chapter we suggested that the idea conveyed by the word in that context is admiration or respect. We find that the word reappears later when there is another flashback. No doubt it is used intentionally in those places to ensure a clear distinction between the beginnings of love in courtship and love consummated in marriage. There is no hint of immorality in the Song, but rather a determination to avoid any risk of misunderstanding on that score.

In verse 7 the young lady wants to know where her fiancé, whom she so greatly appreciates, feeds his flocks and gives them their midday rest, because she is sure that that is where she will find him having his lunchbreak, and she longs to be able to join him there. The question at the end of the verse expresses her heart's desire. No longer does she want to wander in the company of all and sundry: she is desperate for that day when she and her husband-to-be can settle down in married life, and she can be with him all the time in the exclusivity of the marriage relationship.

Behind these comments lies something of a feeling of insecurity. The young lady is longing for the day when she will no longer feel vulnerable in her singleness. In Solomon's day a woman who was unmarried was especially vulnerable. She would have no financial security. Today, that may have changed, but it is still the case that marriage brings a sense of emotional security and safety, for the wife, but also for husband.

And that, surely, is something for which we need to be truly thankful to the Lord. To have a home to return to, a family to belong to, a spouse to cuddle, after the pressures of a day at work, is a great blessing indeed. And we need to take great care not to damage the sense of security in our marriages by careless words or cruel actions.

In verse 8, though, the husband-to-be has no option but to reply that he cannot do anything about it just yet. It is not yet time for them to come together in marriage. They long for this security of togetherness, but he has to say, yes I know you don't want to be mixing with my companions, but there's nothing I can do about it: you've just got to feed your little goats beside the shepherd's tents. You would really like to know where I feed my flocks and give them their midday rest, because you want to be there with me all day, but it's not yet time for us to enter into the inseparability and the security which we shall enjoy once the day of our marriage arrives.

There is a word here, surely, for courting couples. In the first place, notice the seriousness with which this couple approach their courtship. They see it, unquestionably, as a prelude to marriage. I fear that these days some young people see "dating," as it tends to get called in modern parlance, as just a bit of fun on the side, with no commitment involved, no intent awareness that they are preparing for the lifelong challenge of being a married couple. That casual approach to courting is an insult to the Creator, who has made us male and female to become one flesh with our marriage companion. It is a sin which Christian young people must strenuously avoid. And not just young people either, though I suspect that it is more of an issue at that stage of life. But supposing, for example, that a widower and a widow contemplate remarriage after the deaths of their respective spouses, the same commitment to seriousness is demanded even at that later stage in life.

But where there is that biblical understanding of courtship as a solemn prelude to marriage, patience is called for. The temptation to anticipate the wedding day and fall into sin must be vigorously resisted.

But now let us lift our sights again. Let us think of the love of God, and what security there is in that love. In Christ crucified (and his cross is the highest demonstration of the love of God) we are secure on the day of judgement itself, when we are trusting in him to save us. And from that day on we shall be secure for evermore, eternally beyond the reach of harm and danger, of temptation and sin.

Of course, for now, we remain vulnerable. We are vulnerable to the temptations of the devil. We are vulnerable to the pressure from the world to conform to its ways. We are vulnerable to the instincts of our own sinful flesh. Consequently, our hearts ache for that day when we shall be with Christ. There is a longing within us for that consummation of our union with our Savior, because, as 1 John 3:2 reminds us, "we know that when he is revealed, we shall be like him, for we shall see him as he is." At least, I hope that we know that aching heart. I trust that we have not become so accustomed to life in a fallen world that we have lost our expectancy, our anticipation, of the better world to come. I hope that we have not lost our hope, that we do press forward from day to day with that genuine, confident assurance lifting our spirits that we shall at last "always be with the Lord," as Paul puts it in 1 Thessalonians 4:17.

I trust that our attitude, as we love our Savior and long to be with him, is truly summed up by these lines from James Montgomery's hymn:

> Forever with the Lord! Amen! so let it be.
> Life from the dead is in that word, 'tis immortality.
> Here in the body pent, absent from him, I roam,
> Yet nightly pitch my moving tent a day's march nearer home.
>
> My Father's house on high, home of my soul, how near
> At times to faith's foreseeing eye thy golden gates appear!
> Ah, then my spirit faints to reach the land I love,
> The bright inheritance of saints, Jerusalem above!
>
> Forever with the Lord! Father, if 'tis thy will,
> The promise of that faithful word e'en here to me fulfil.
> Be thou at my right hand, then can I never fail.
> Uphold thou me, and I shall stand; fight, and I must prevail.
>
> So when my dying breath shall set my spirit free,
> By death I shall escape from death to endless life with thee.
> Knowing as I am known; how shall I love that word
> And oft repeat before the throne, "Forever with the Lord!"[1]

In the meantime, patience is demanded of us. From James 5:7, we receive the exhortation, "be patient, brethren, until the coming of the Lord." In Romans 2:7 the Lord promises "eternal life to those who by patient continuance in doing good seek for glory, honor,

---

1. James Montgomery (1771–1854).

and immortality." And in Hebrews 6:11–12 he expresses his desire for each one of us: that "you show the same diligence to the full assurance of hope until the end, that you do not become sluggish, but imitate those who through faith and patience inherit the promises." Yes, we shall inherit the promises in due time provided that we endure to the end, that we do not fall away, and it is our love for the Lord, and our joy in his love for us that will keep us pressing forward towards that glorious day when we shall be fully embraced in the love of Christ.

4

Beauty Affirmed

(Song of Solomon 1:9–16a)

We come now to the next song in this song-cycle, which runs from verse 9 as far as the second line of verse 16, finishing with the words, "Yes, pleasant!" We now return to the situation where Solomon and Shulamite are a well-established married couple. The theme in these verses we might call the beautifying affirmation of married love.

Once again we are listening in to a conversation between the husband and the wife. He speaks in verses 9–11, and then she responds in verses 12–14. The husband speaks again in verse 15, and the wife in this first part of verse 16.

When you read this passage, you could form the impression that this couple have started a mutual admiration society! They are flattering each other with various expressions. But then, when you think about it, isn't that just what marriage is? It is certainly to be hoped that a husband and wife admire each other. How tragic if, with the passing of the years, contempt for each other were to set in. We must never lose respect for each other within marriage. But if we want respect, we had better behave so that we deserve it. And it is good to put our feelings into words, just like Solomon and Shulamite do here.

So here the husband speaks first. He compares his wife to one of the horses pulling Pharaoh's chariots. Perhaps you have seen a shire horse at an agricultural show. They decorate the shire horses with all sorts of colorful ornaments. That is the kind of thing that is being referred to here. In verse 10 Solomon is imagining the elegance of a horse when it is covered with all these things that make its beauty so much the greater. Now in verse 11, he makes a suggestion to his wife. He has spoken in verse 10 of ornaments and strings of beads in general terms. Now he suggests going one better and making them of gold and silver. And what lies behind the suggestion is the thought, you are far more beautiful than the best of Pharaoh's horses, however elegantly decorated they may be. They have just got any old ornaments, any old beads, but your beauty, my wife, is gold and silver, second to none. In fact you are more beautiful than anyone or anything else that can be found anywhere in this world.

It is interesting how Solomon says, "We will make you ornaments of gold." He emphasizes their joint involvement in this project. There is a sense in which love creates beauty. A woman who is loved by her husband develops elegance, not just outwardly, but in personality and character as well. By loving and respecting his wife, a husband makes her all the more precious. He turns all the ornamentation in her character into gold.

And now the wife responds in verse 12. We learn now that they are sitting at the table: the two of them are having a special private meal together towards the end of the day. The day's duties are finished, and now the evening meal is her opportunity to share with her husband her love for him. So she has put on some of the best perfume that she possesses.

After the meal, in verses 13 and 14, we find them embracing one another in their love. Shulamite mentions myrrh in verse 13. In those days myrrh used to be worn by women around their necks in a little pouch. Myrrh was a solid substance, a bit like wax. As it hung there the heat of the body gradually melted it down and released the fragrance. What she is saying as she snuggles up to her husband is that the pleasure of his presence gradually increases the more she enjoys it. The fragrance of delight in being together slowly builds up, just as the myrrh gradually gives off its scent.

In verse 14 she goes on to speak of henna blooms. Henna was a yellow plant which was used as a dye. Women would use it as a nail varnish in those days. What Shulamite is suggesting is that in their togetherness, the husband's influence pervades his wife. He has become like a dye stamping his character and personality on her. She feels that he is the best of the best: En Gedi was the place where the very best henna grew in Palestine.

In verses 15 and 16 each one tells the other how beautiful, how handsome, they are. The husband sees beauty shining out of the eyes of his wife. And she finds her husband so pleasant to be with. It is these affirmations which they make to each other which create and enhance their beauty.

We all need to be affirmed, to be praised, encouraged, commended, approved. If you are constantly being put down you become soured inside. Your personality becomes unpleasant. But regular doses of affirmation and encouragement make you feel sweet inside, and your personality comes out as a beautiful thing. We need to learn, in our marriages, to affirm one another, and so to make one another the more beautiful. The husband must overcome his reticence, and every day tell his wife how wonderful, how appreciated she is.

It is a good practice, on a regular basis, to have a special private meal together, just like Solomon and Shulamite are doing here. If there are just the two of you, that happens automatically every day, I guess. But when you have got a family, it is good to get the children to bed (or at least out of the way) a bit earlier, perhaps once a week, so that husband and wife can share a meal that is just for the two of them. But when we do, let's not waste the time. Let's use it as an opportunity to affirm one another and to delight in one another's company.

There is wisdom here for us in the way that myrrh gradually and increasingly releases its sweet smell. It takes time to build up a depth of relationship. It is a never-ending process, a lifelong process, which continues throughout the years of marriage. How dangerous if we become neglectful of these precious times together, if we stop commending and praising and expressing appreciation for our loved one. How terrible if, after a couple of decades as a married couple we just start taking each other for granted. God's word challenges us here with the reminder of the need to be affirming, to express love in words and actions truly "until death us do part." If it is true that our influence makes its stamp on our spouse's personality, let's seek God's grace that what pervades may truly be godly and beautiful.

And now, when you look heavenwards, you find that God is just the same. The God who loves us is not for ever slamming us for our faults and failings. He tells us in Ephesians 1:6 that we are "accepted in the Beloved." He embraces us in the Lord Jesus. He affirms us for who we are as made in the image of God, and as remade in the image of Christ. The Psalmist makes a thrilling statement in Psalm 149:4, where he writes, "the LORD . . . will beautify the humble with salvation."

When the Lord gave Moses the instructions for making the garments for the priesthood, he gave these two explanations in Exodus 28 verses 2 and 40: "you shall make holy garments for Aaron your brother, for glory and for beauty," and "for Aaron's sons you shall make tunics, and you shall make sashes for them. And you shall make hats for them, for glory and beauty."

In 1 Peter 2:5 we read, "you also, as living stones, are being built up a spiritual house, a holy priesthood." Then verse 9 adds: "you are a chosen generation, a royal priesthood, a holy nation, his own special people." And God, our loving Savior, has provided for us too garments for beauty. This is how the work of Jesus, the Lord's anointed, is prophesied in Isaiah 61:3: he comes "to console those who mourn in Zion, to give them beauty for ashes, the oil of joy for mourning, the garment of praise for the spirit of heaviness; that they may be called trees of righteousness, the planting of the LORD, that he may be glorified." In Psalm 45:11 we hear these words, again prophetic of Christ's outlook on his people: "the King will greatly desire your beauty." In Psalm 50:2 God describes Zion, symbolizing his people, as "the perfection of beauty."

Perhaps we find it amazing that the Lord should regard us in this way—and so it is, but that makes it not one bit less true. And this higher element in the Song of Solomon helps us to grasp something of the wonder of our Savior's love for us.

But, of course, it is not all one way. In these verses of the Song, Solomon and Shulamite are indeed admiring each other. And just as Jesus admires us, his people, and affirms his love for us, so we must never be embarrassed to tell him that we love him. Are we accustomed to flattering Jesus in our prayers? Actually, you cannot really flatter him, because the highest praise of which we are capable inevitably falls far short of the praise of which he is worthy. Isaiah 33:17 looks forward to a day when "your eyes will see the King in his beauty." When we do see him, when he comes again as King of kings and Lord of lords, we shall certainly be enraptured by the beauty of Jesus. We shall find that it far surpasses our highest imagination.

In the meantime, we are called to share David's sentiment which he expresses in Psalm 27:4:

> One thing I have desired of the LORD,
> That will I seek:
> That I may dwell in the house of the LORD
> All the days of my life,
> To behold the beauty of the LORD.

We are called to "worship the LORD in the beauty of holiness," a phrase which recurs several times, for example in Psalm 96:9. And as 2 Chronicles 20:21 makes clear, it is pre-eminently his beauty which is in view. That verse reads like this: "And when he [that is Jehoshaphat] had consulted with the people, he appointed those who should sing to the LORD, and who should praise the beauty of holiness, as they went out before the army and were saying: 'Praise the LORD, for his mercy endures forever.'" And there is the most staggeringly attractive beauty which the Lord possesses, the beauty of his mercy.

In this section of the Song of Solomon we glimpsed Solomon and Shulamite sharing a meal together. That reminds us that we, too, have a love feast which we celebrate with our Lord. Let us make sure that we never fall into the trap of regarding Holy Communion as merely symbolic. It is symbolic, of course. The bread and the wine remain bread and wine, representing the body and blood of Christ, but not undergoing any change of substance. But the Lord's Supper is sacramental.

The term "sacrament" seems to have dropped out of usage in some circles in recent years, but it has been the normal term throughout church history. It is a term which is vitally significant. It was borrowed from Roman military usage, where it meant the oath by which a soldier bound himself to be faithful to his general, and not to become a deserter. In a similar way, as we partake of the sacramental ordinance we are committing ourselves to follow Christ wherever he leads. But we go beyond the secular use of the term. There is more to it than the cold commitment to a military captain. The sacrament in Christian worship truly is a love feast. As we participate, we are renewing our pledge to love our Savior with all our hearts. And he is present in a unique way at Holy Communion. It is an occasion when our heartfelt communion with him is underlined and strengthened, when our unity with him as our heavenly lover is sealed, as, alongside our physical eating and drinking, in our hearts, by faith, we genuinely feed upon the living bread, who is Christ himself, and find that our love for him grows, and our union with him deepens.

So these verses from the Song of Solomon remind us of the mutual love which there is between the Savior and his people. Truly, we make our own the words of 1 Peter 2:7, which says, "to you who believe, he is precious." And we receive the Lord's response, which we read in Isaiah 43:4, "Since you were precious in my sight, you have been honored, and I have loved you."

5

A Love Duet: Luxury and Specialness

(Song of Solomon 1:16b—2:3a)

In 1982 Sir James Galway, the flute player, co-wrote a book with William Mann to accompany a television series which he presented. It was entitled *Music in Time*. In that book it says that "man's first songs were celebratory."[1] The Song of Solomon is basically a celebration of God's wonderful gift to men and women of love in marriage. As we sing along with this Song we are celebrating married love, and also being led upwards to the even more glorious celebration of the eternal love of God for his people in Christ.

Back in 1979 Yehudi Menuhin, the violinist, wrote a book, along with Curtis Davis, called *The Music of Man*. He tells us there that the idea of love songs emerged in western Europe in the thirteenth century. He describes the kind of songs which appeared back then as "earthy and passionate."[2]

Well, the Song of Solomon is a love song, and it managed to beat western Europe by a good two thousand years. But it is just as

1. Mann and Galway, *Music in Time*, 14.
2. Menuhin and Davis, *Music of Man*, 61.

passionate and just as earthy. But we have been seeing how the description of the passionate, earthly love between Solomon and Shulamite also points us upwards to the love of God for his people in Christ, and so sends us right back down to earth again to celebrate love in the context of marriage with all the passion of that love.

Another thing that Yehudi Menuhin mentions is that in the century after the love song first appeared in western Europe—in the fourteenth century—love duets started being sung for the first time on this continent. His comment reads like this: "It was possible now for the voices of a man and woman to join in singing the praises of the pangs and rewards of love."[3]

Well, yet again the Song of Solomon had the same idea many centuries sooner. In the passage that we are considering now we have a love duet—Solomon and Shulamite singing together of love, and especially of its rewards. They rejoice together in what every marriage might be by the grace of God. It is an idealized picture, full of imagery. But it is a target, which we should all be aiming at in our married lives.

The first theme which emerges from this passage is this:

MARRIED LOVE MAKES LIFE LUXURIOUS (1:16B–17).

In these verses both Solomon and Shulamite speak together in unison. They begin to sing a duet, and this first part of the duet is about the luxury of their home.

They tell us that their house was built of cedar and that it had a roof made of the wood of the fir tree. In those days, if that was true, it meant that you were living in the lap of luxury. Wood of any kind was so very expensive that it was only ever found in palaces and temples. Cedar was the most expensive wood of all. Of course, Solomon and his wife did live in a palace, and, in fact, we notice that the word "houses" is plural: they were sufficiently well off to own more than one place. But that is not the main point that they

3. Menuhin and Davis, *Music of Man*, 63.

are making. What these lines are really getting at is that love will transform the meanest hovel into the most lavish castle.

In the USA they pride themselves on the fact that some of the men who have become President had a poor upbringing. They have the saying "from log cabin to White House." Well, marriage will make a White House of any log cabin. It will make a Buckingham Palace of a terraced house. Love turns life into something luxurious. That is the point that is being made. The whole world is green, to refer to the last line of verse 16: in other words, it is bursting with life, when you are in love.

We remember that feeling from our early days of courtship, do we not? Everything seemed so wonderful! But why ever stop? Why not luxuriate all life long, throughout marriage? There is no reason why it should be true only of courting days.

Do you sometimes wish that you had a better house, or more money, or a greater number of life's luxuries? When that is not possible, what is the best answer? This—just keep on falling in love with your husband, your wife. Then the whole of life will become luxurious, and your heart will be comforted. Proverbs 15:17 says, "Better is a dinner of herbs where love is, than a fatted calf with hatred."

And God's love is luxurious. Let's just take the three key words from this duet, and see how they are developed elsewhere in Scripture. The first key word is "green." In the last line of verse 16 Solomon and Shulamite celebrate the greenness of their marital home. And David says in Psalm 23:2, "He makes me to lie down in green pastures." Admittedly, a different Hebrew word for "green" is used here, but the point is similar. Listen to what Albert Barnes says about those words:

> The idea . . . is that of flocks that lie down on the grass "fully fed" or "satisfied," their wants being completely supplied. The exact point of contemplation in the mind of the poet . . . is that of a flock in young and luxuriant grass, surrounded by abundance, and, having satisfied their wants, lying down amidst this luxuriance with calm contentment. It is not merely a flock enjoying repose; it is a flock whose wants are supplied, lying down in the midst

of abundance. Applied to the psalmist himself, or to the people of God generally, the idea is, that the wants of the soul are met and satisfied, and that, in the full enjoyment of this, there is the conviction of abundance—the repose of the soul at present satisfied, and feeling that in such abundance want will always be unknown.[4]

That is our joy in the love of our Lord.

The second key word is "cedar." When Balak asked Balaam to curse the Israelites, the Lord intervened and prevented Balaam from complying with Balak's request. Instead, Balaam was compelled to pronounce God's blessing on his people. His words of blessing included this statement in Numbers 24:5–6: "How lovely are your tents, O Jacob! your dwellings, O Israel! Like valleys that stretch out, like gardens by the riverside, like aloes planted by the LORD, like cedars beside the waters." The cedar is seen here as the epitome of loveliness, "an image of majestic beauty," as Barnes puts it. Matthew Henry also comments on the beauty that Balaam can here discern in God's people: "Though they dwelt not in stately palaces, but in coarse and homely tents, and these, no doubt, sadly weather beaten, yet Balaam sees a beauty in those tents."

God's people, embraced in his love, "are compared to the beauty and sweetness of fruitful valleys and fine gardens, flourishing trees and fragrant spices," as Matthew Henry continues.[5] Even though our earthly situation may be very rundown, in Christ we possess a luxuriant beauty.

But it is equally true that, to us, our Savior is also the epitome of luxuriant beauty. Our third key word is "fir." In Hosea 14:8, the Lord speaks like this to his people, restored after backsliding: "I am like a green cypress tree; your fruit is found in me." The word there translated "cypress" is almost the same as the word translated "fir" in our text.

The fir tree is an evergreen, which depicts unchanging freshness. Regarding this tree, Barnes observes that its wood was "precious enough to be employed in the temple; fine enough to be used

---

4. Barnes, *Notes,* loc. 66317.

5. Henry, *Commentary,* on Num. 24:1–9.

in all sorts of musical instruments; strong and pliant enough to be used for spears."[6] And in fellowship with our Savior, we dwell in a house not made with hands, a precious house of fine excellence, a strong house where we dwell safely in the luxury of his love.

John Gill comments on the Lord's words through Hosea here that Christ may be compared to a fir tree because it is "a choice one, as he is to his Father, and to all believers, chosen and precious, lovely and beloved." Gill continues:

> Christ is most amiable, and altogether lovely to look at in his person and fulness; and he looks in a loving, smiling manner upon his people; . . . and as this tree, as here, is ever green, so he is always the same; he ever lives, and his people in him, and by him; his fulness always continues to supply them.[7]

These things characterize our relationship with Jesus now: to be loved by him, and to love him who first loved us, is to live a life of spiritual luxury, which the less luxurious aspects of earthly existence cannot alter. But in the end, we might say, the Lord is going to build a house of cedar and fir for his people in heaven. Jesus assures us in John 14:2 that he is preparing a mansion for us. Whatever accommodation we may have grown used to on earth, when we get to glory, the luxury of heaven will far surpass the best that we have enjoyed here below. And to be caught up into the eternal love of God will cause the best of life's experiences to pale into insignificance.

So married love makes life luxurious. And now follows the theme of the second love duet in this passage:

MARRIED LOVE MAKES YOU SPECIAL (2:1–3A).

The duet now takes a slightly different form. At the end of chapter 1 the married couple were singing together in unison. Here the wife and her husband sing in turn. She begins in verse 1, he responds in verse 2, and we hear her words again in the first two lines of verse 3.

6. Barnes, *Notes*, loc. 169382.
7. Gill, *Exposition*, on Hos. 14:8.

They are not speaking to anyone in particular, but just describing to each other, or to the world at large, how they see each other within the love of their marriage.

In the first verse the wife declares her own beauty, by comparison with a rose and a lily. The rose and Sharon are mentioned also in Isaiah 35:1–2. There we read, "The desert shall rejoice and blossom as a rose," and a few lines later we hear of "the excellence of Carmel and Sharon." A rose blossoms, and Sharon is marked by excellence. And Shulamite describes herself as "the rose of Sharon," a rose blossoming with excellence. The lily is found in Hosea 14:5. Here God says, "I will be like the dew to Israel; he shall grow like the lily." So the lily speaks of growth. Taking the two flowers together, we have a picture of growth in blossoming excellence, growth in beauty. The wife is conscious that she is growing in beauty day by day.

Well, we might ask, isn't that a bit conceited? But the answer is: not at all. She is musing on her husband's words to her. She has heard him declare how beautiful she is, and how her beauty blossoms abundantly as the years pass. She is reveling in what she has heard him say to her.

Then in verse 2 we actually hear him say it. The husband pictures an ugly scene. Thorn bushes are growing everywhere. But then he says, look, here in the middle is this solitary lily, stupendous in beauty, and all the more abundant in its beauty because of the contrast with its surroundings. Here is a husband who is aware that we live in an ugly world, where there is so much sin, so much pain. Thorns, we remember from Genesis 3:18, are one of the main indicators that we are now living in a world under God's curse because of sin. But what prevents Solomon from giving way to utter despair as he looks at such a world? Well, it is that he is able to set his eye on this object of spectacular beauty in the middle of it all—his wife. And she really is so special.

In verse 3 she responds. If she is unique in beauty for him, then he is incomparable in excellence for her. She speaks of "the woods," a scene of haphazard growth. But there in the middle of the woods someone has planted an apple tree, a fruit tree. And it is so special to have the opportunity to feed on fruit in such a setting.

If you are familiar with Kenneth Grahame's story, *The Wind in the Willows,* you will be aware of the wild wood. The animals hate to go into the wild wood, because it's damp, it's dark, it's full of fear, there are strange noises. And the wife is aware that this world can be a dark, fearsome place. But in her husband she finds one whose presence is fruitful, nourishing, comforting, one who is special to her just because she is special to him. The wife is not just some nondescript piece of vegetation. She is like a lily. And the husband is not just any old tree. He is an apple tree.

Sylvia Hubbard was a member of a church in Hull which I pastored in the late 1980's. She was then in her 60's, a widow. I was single at the time. I once had a conversation with her in which she commended marriage to me. I always remember what she said. She said: "Marriage makes you special." She had picked up just the theme which Solomon presents to us here. When you are married there is one person for whom you are the only person who matters in all the world.

There is a challenge here to those of us who are husbands. Is your wife able to muse on her own beauty, because she has learned from you just how special she is, through the tender words you speak and the considerate actions you perform?

And perhaps there is a challenge for the wives as well. Do you ensure that your husband truly realizes that, despite all the demands which life throws at you, you find life fruitful, because of his love for you?

And so we are pointed upwards from married love to the fact that "God so loved the world that he gave his only begotten Son." What a dignity of specialness God conferred on this poor world of thorns when he loved like that!

And truly, Jesus finds us beautiful. To him we are incredibly special. Addressing wives in 1 Peter 3, the apostle urges them not to be over-bothered about outward beauty, not to prioritize things like hairstyle, jewelry, and clothing; he then says in verse 4, "rather let it be the hidden person of the heart, with the incorruptible beauty of a gentle and quiet spirit, which is very precious in the sight of God." And the Lord Jesus finds incorruptible beauty in his bride, the church. That spirit of quiet gentleness or gentle quietness means so much to the Lord, because it is the fruit of his Spirit's working in our lives, changing us to resemble him.

And that inner working of grace makes the church so special to Jesus Christ. Yes, we do live in an ugly, sinful, cursed world. But to Jesus his church stands out! In his people he sees a bright gem in that dark setting.

And, of course, Jesus is special to us. We find in him, as Shulamite did in her husband, the source of everything that is fruitful. And what a comforting reality it is in a fallen world to know the Savior's marvelous love for us.

6

Stronger Together

(Song of Solomon 2:3b–6)

The love duet has celebrated how married love makes life luxurious and makes you special. At this point the duet comes to a close, and now we hear just the wife speaking. The theme which runs through this passage is that married love gives you strength.

For most of the section the wife is musing, talking to herself about her experience of love, enjoying both the memory and the present reality of her husband's love. But in verse 5 she speaks directly to her husband.

In the second part of verse 3 we are being taken in our imagination to a hot, sunny day, a dry day in summer. What is going to bring you delight on a day like that? It is too hot to sunbathe. So you are going to look for a seat in the shade with a cool glass of fruit juice to refresh you. And it is just that sort of reviving refreshment which the wife finds in her husband's love, as she expresses her delight in these words:

> I sat down in his shadow with great delight,
> And his fruit *was* sweet to my taste.

In verse 4 she continues to express the same thought, but this time using a different picture. Now we are sitting, not in the shade of a tree, but inside the banqueting house. Literally, it means an inn, the Costa Express of those days, the place where travelers can find refreshment on their journey. So the wife is saying, on this wearying journey through life there is a place where I find refreshment—in the love of my husband.

She says, "his banner over me was love." A banner is a flag. When Amundsen reached the South Pole he stuck a flag in it. When Tenzing and Hilary reached the summit of Everest they stuck a flag on the top of the mountain. It was a way of saying, "we possess this territory because we were the first to reach it." The husband has a flag of possession upon his wife, and the flag is love.

And in that love the wife finds refreshment and sustenance, as verse 5 indicates. In this verse she is calling her husband to come and express his love to her. The imagery of raisin cakes and apples speaks of thoroughgoing satisfaction. They represent the best, the sweetest, the most satisfying foods. Shulamite says, "I am lovesick." She is longing desperately for her husband's gentle embrace, because in his love she finds sweet refreshment and deep satisfaction equal to that of the choicest food. She finds in his love a refreshing sustenance comparable to what she gets from her favorite delicacies. Her husband responds, and in verse 6 we have a description of the wife's desire fulfilled, as he expresses his love for her.

Marriage is indeed a great source of strength. Life in this world can be severely trying. In different ways it is for nearly every one of us. We feel that the heat is turned up, and we get breathless with the pace of the world. It feels as if we are careering along the road of life, and we are desperate for the refreshing sustenance of sweet and enjoyable experiences. When you are on your own, you may be prone to depression. You may feel that you have no resilience to face all these challenges and trials that make up everyday life.

And God's gift of marriage is the greatest source at the human level of sweet, sustaining, refreshing reinvigoration. "Two are better than one," we read in Ecclesiastes 4:9. When you are alongside your loved one there are resources in your togetherness which you never knew were available when you were single. And there again is a cause of great thankfulness to the Creator who made us male and female, with the possibility of becoming one flesh, and finding each in the other the resources that transform life's challenges and that sustain us through life's trials.

Perhaps we husbands need to be challenged again right here. We are listening in these verses to a wife's musings on the strength and refreshment she finds in her husband's love. I hope that my wife can muse like that! Each of us needs to ask ourself, is my love of such a quality that my wife finds it sweet and sustaining? Just think of the hot situations in life that a wife has to face—the trials of womanhood, of motherhood (or, in some cases, of the inability to have children), of home-making, the frustrated ambitions, the balancing of responsibilities, the cares that are part of a woman's experience of life. How she needs to be embraced and supported and caressed and loved so tenderly! I hope that we husbands today, like the husband in the Song, are ready to respond to our wives when they need our reassurance. I hope that we fly the banner of love, the flag of loving possession and commitment, over our wives. I do not think that our wives want to live under a flag of possessiveness that comes out as power and demand. But if it is the possessiveness of loving esteem, the banner of love, I am pretty sure that they will welcome that. So let's all make sure that that is the flag that flies over our homes.

And now, of course, the Song of Solomon urges us to turn our sights upwards. It is just so to be loved by God. He is the source of the greatest possible strength. In the love of our Lord we find that sustaining refreshment that Shulamite longed for in her husband, and in Christ we find it to an incomparably greater degree than is possible in the very best of human relationships. Human marriage proves to be a signpost to that greatest love of all.

Shulamite longs for the sustaining love of her husband. The Greek word used in the Septuagint for "sustain" in verse 5 appears a number of times in the New Testament of the Lord's power to establish us, his people. It comes twice in the space of a few verses in 2 Thessalonians 2:16–17 and 3:3. Listen to those three verses:

> Now may our Lord Jesus Christ himself, and our God
> and Father, who has loved us and given us everlasting

> consolation and good hope by grace, comfort your hearts
> and establish you in every good word and work . . . . The
> Lord is faithful, who will establish you and guard you
> from the evil one.

The context here is similar to what we found in our passage from the Song of Solomon. This world is challenging; the evil one is rampant; the heat of trial burns down on you. To fulfil the good words and works of our calling is demanding. We need to be comforted and encouraged constantly. We need to be protected from descending into hopeless despair. But we are not on our own. It is our Lord who will establish us, or sustain us, through the trials of the Christian pathway. And at the root of his sustaining grace is the truth that he has loved us. And notice the apostle's turn of phrase: "our Lord Jesus Christ himself." This is not a task which he delegates to someone else. When you look to the cross, you realize that he "himself bore our sins in his own body on the tree," to quote 1 Peter 2:24. You know that God loved you while you were still a sinner, and so you know that in his passionate love for his people, he is at our side, and truly we find strength in his love, and refreshment for our souls in meditating on that wonderful love.

7

"The Winter is Past"

(Song of Solomon 2:7–3:5)

The first and last verses of this passage (2:7 and 3:5) are identical. This is a word of warning, voiced at the beginning and then repeated at the end. Chapter 2 verse 15 is another word of warning in the middle of the passage.

In this chapter we shall look at the rest of the section, and then return in the next chapter to these warnings. There are three main themes in the larger parts of the passage, all of which revolve around the truth that married love brings to an end the winter of loneliness. The first theme can be summarized like this:

MARRIED LOVE PUTS A SPRING IN YOUR STEP (2:8-14).

Here we have another of those passages where the wife is musing. Verses 10-13 are actually the words of her husband, but, as the first line of verse 10 makes clear, she is quoting him.

I have to confess that in choosing the heading for this section I am using a pun. The imagery in these verses is all about spring. Spring is in the air when people are in love. And especially in the words of her husband, which the wife is recalling and quoting to herself, there is an emphasis on spring. Notice in verse 11, "the winter is past." The rainy season has finished.

Perhaps with our western climate we are as used to it raining in spring as at any other time of year. But in the countries of the east, there is a definite rainy season, which lasts for several months. It rains constantly.

My wife and I experienced the rainy season when we spent three months in the Philippines back in the year 2000 when I taught for one semester at Grace Ministerial Academy in Manila. The semester opened just as the rainy season was beginning. It rained torrentially. The streets were like rivers. To go shopping you had to wade through the water. The one saving grace was that the weather was very warm, so you got wet through, but then dried out in next to no time. But then the rainy season finishes. It stops raining, and you do not see another drop of rain until next year.

And that is the sort of picture that is in the writer's mind here in Song of Solomon 2:11. And this awareness that springtime has arrived gives the wife a real thrill.

In verse 8 and the first line of verse 9 Shulamite is reveling in Solomon's loving advances towards her, and longing that there should be a repetition of the experience. She is on her own as she speaks. Solomon is busy about the affairs of state, but she knows that he will be back in due course, and she anticipates him coming leaping, skipping, dancing towards her like a young deer. 2 Samuel 2:18 tells us that a wild gazelle is "fleet of foot," and 1 Chronicles 12:8 says that a gazelle is "swift . . . on the mountains." And Solomon will be full of joy at the sight of his wife again after the pressures of a demanding day. And in her anticipation, Shulamite gets excited, because she knows that his playful skip says that he is excited too.

The rest of verse 9 finds the husband gazing lovingly into the windows of his wife's eyes, staring through the lattice of her eyelashes.

In verses 10–13 she remembers the kind of thing he says to her so regularly in this playfulness of love. There is the invitation in verse 10 to be alone together:

Rise up, my love, my fair one,
And come away.

The invitation is repeated at the end of verse 13: it brackets the section, which indicates that these verses as a whole are an elaborate invitation to spend time together in the solitude of mutual love. So in verse 11 it is springtime, because married love turns life into a permanent spring. The winter is past—that winter of singleness—it is over. The rains—the tears of loneliness—are finished with, over and gone for good. When you are in love with your spouse you feel that the world is ablaze with color, full of blossoming flowers. Music is in the air: it is time to sing, and to enjoy hearing the singing of the birds. Verse 12 tells us all that, and then the first part of verse 13 affirms that everything seems green and young and fragrant, because married love has transforming power.

Two things especially are worth noting in these verses. First, apparently the turtledove, mentioned in verse 12, is unique in Palestine. Most birds there sing the dawn chorus and then remain silent until the next morning. The turtledove is different: it sings all day. When you are married you feel like singing all the time. Love turns the whole of life into a permanent spring-song.

Second, turning to verse 13, the fig tree and the vine are regular biblical symbols of peace and security. This song is written by Solomon. When he was king the nation of Israel was at the peak of its success. At that time, we read, "Judah and Israel dwelt safely, each man under his vine and his fig tree" (1 Kings 4:25). Here is the reason why marriage is a lifelong experience of music and play that puts a spring in your step: you are safe and secure in mutual love.

In verse 14 we find the couple in the secret place, able to enjoy the loving togetherness which she has been anticipating.

So a vision is being held up to us of what marriage ought to be, and of what it may be by the grace of God. We husbands and wives should be enraptured with one another, longing for one another, excited by one another. We husbands should look forward with elation to being in the refreshing presence of our wives again, whenever duty has taken us away, and placed its demands upon our shoulders. Husband and wife together may find life colorful, musical, fresh—a permanent springtime, that truly puts a spring in our step.

In our marriages we must never lose this carefree sense of fun in being in love with each other. We remember it well when we first fell in love. What a spring there was in our step then! How we used to run together down the slopes and up the hills! What effusive silliness there was in simply being together and enjoying each other! And why should it ever be different just because we have now been married for so many years?

But then we remember that marriage is a reflection of God's love for his people. There is joy in knowing that you are loved by God, and the joy of love in marriage is an earthly reflection of that heavenly love. This passage depicts the wife thrilling to her beloved's dance towards her, reveling in his closeness, longing for that seclusion where she is alone in his presence, and can hear his colorful expressions of love to her, the music of his charming voice.

We are reminded of our Savior's delight in his people today, and our response is to long for him. Are we really longing for that day when we shall finally see him in all his glory? And are we ensuring that right now we "spend much time in secret with Jesus alone," to quote the words of William Longstaff from his hymn, "Take time to be holy"?[1]

And if married life on earth turns the drabbest periods into a springtime, and puts a spring in our step, even through life's troubles and difficulties, then how much more uplifting is our experience of God's love in the Lord Jesus Christ! How refreshed we are by his presence. "Times of refreshing" shall "come from the presence of the Lord" (Acts 3:19).

The turtledove, referred to in verse 12, is used also in Psalm 74:19 to represent God's people. We read there, "Oh, do not deliver the life of your turtledove to the wild beast! Do not forget the life of your poor forever." J. A. Alexander speaks here of the turtledove as "an expression of affectionate endearment."[2] That is how the Lord sees you and me. We are precious to him. We are dear to him. He

1. William Dunn Longstaff (1822–94).
2. Alexander, *Psalms*, 317.

has great and deep affection for us. May we revel in his love just as Shulamite did in Solomon's.

So married love puts a spring in your step. Moving on, we come to our second theme:

MARRIED LOVE BRINGS SATISFACTION (2:16–17).

In this section the wife is still speaking. In verse 16 we find her once again in her musing mode, just enjoying her feelings and her memory of love. In verse 17 she speaks directly to her husband.

The first line of verse 16, "my beloved is mine and I am his," says that the wife finds it a fully satisfying experience to be in love with a faithful husband. The second line adds that there is satisfaction for the husband too in being married to his wife.

We notice that the words "his flock" are in italics in the New King James Version. That indicates that they were not present in the original text. Sometimes the translators have to insert words to make the translation flow better in English. But those words are not part of the inspired word of God, and it is possible sometimes that the translators have distorted the meaning by adding them. I think that might be the case here. "He feeds among the lilies," is what the wife says:[3] he is fed by the love that they share, so precious to him is his wife, who is now compared to lilies. Back in verse 2 the husband described his wife as a single lily, resplendent in beauty in the midst of a world of ugly thorns. Well now she is not a solitary lily, but a bunch of lilies: she is not just resplendent, but exuberant, in beauty.

The particular word for lily used in both verses in this chapter "appears mainly in poetic material as a symbol of beauty."[4] Shulamite knows that her husband is entranced by her beauty. He is even nurtured in his inner being through contemplating his wife.

Perhaps it is significant too that the Hebrew word for "lily" is based on the word for "joy." Verse 16 is telling us of the mutual joy that this couple find in their marriage. The exclusive devotion which marriage entails leads to satisfaction for both. So in verse

3. See Gledhill, *Message*, 141.
4. Wolf, *Lily*, 914.

17 the wife invites her husband to come as fast as he can, with the speed and playfulness of the deer in the mountains, and then to stay at her side the whole night long.

As married couples, we must foster this eager togetherness, each one seeking to satisfy the other. Then for both, the cup of joy will be full and overflowing. The wife has spoken these two verses, and her words are a challenge to us men to be like her husband, as she describes him here—to be eager for the company of our wives, not at all just to take them for granted. And that will make our wives as happy as Shulamite was. Then we men in turn will be happy too.

But let us lift our sights once more. Human love is so satisfying because it is an image of the love of Jesus. He says to his people in John 6:35, "I am the bread of life." Bread satisfies, and Jesus Christ brings eternal satisfaction to the soul. In marriage we get a preview of that eternal fullness.

And just as Solomon finds Shulamite to be the precious lily which is the source of all his joy, so there is a mutual rejoicing in each other between Christ and his bride, his church. So we can say, in the words of Isaiah 61:10,

> I will greatly rejoice in the LORD,
> My soul shall be joyful in my God;
> For he has clothed me with the garments of salvation,
> He has covered me with the robe of righteousness,
> As a bridegroom decks himself with ornaments,
> And as a bride adorns herself with her jewels.

And just as we rejoice greatly in the Lord, so the Lord rejoices in us, his people. I love these words from Zephaniah 3:17:

> The LORD your God in your midst,
> The Mighty One, will save;
> He will rejoice over you with gladness,
> He will quiet you with his love,
> He will rejoice over you with singing.

In heaven we shall be able to say of Christ, "My beloved is mine and I am his." There will then be such togetherness between Christ and his bride. But, of course, we can say it already, because in our souls we get a foretaste of the love that will be revealed to us in all its splendor when we finally see Christ face-to-face.

So we have seen that married love puts a spring in your step, and that married love brings satisfaction. And now our final theme for this section is that

MARRIED LOVE ENDS THE
DESPERATION OF WAITING (3:1–4).

Ariel and Chana Bloch are a Jewish couple, who have written a book on the Song of Solomon. It includes a fresh translation of the Song along with a commentary on it from a Jewish perspective. In that book they make this comment: "Shakespeare was right about lovers: they have such seething brains, such fantasies. To be in love is to be caught up in the power of fantasy."[5]

As Song of Solomon 3 begins, we find Shulamite fantasizing or dreaming. We are back in the days before she was married to Solomon, and we find her consumed by a desperate desire to be married. She feels that she cannot wait any longer. Night after night there is only one thought in her mind—her beloved. She is looking for him. She says that twice in verse 1. The tense of the verb suggests great intensity, and the repetition demonstrates just how desperate she is for her beloved, how she wishes she could have him with her now. But she cannot find him yet: they are not married. The time has not yet come when they can be together day and night.

It could be that this is a dream, or it may be that she is so consumed by her longing that she cannot sleep, and lies awake letting her imagination run riot. Either way, she is feeling this desperation of a waiting love.

In verses 2–3 we find Shulamite, this young, unmarried woman, getting up (only in her dream or her imagination), and going out into the streets and squares of the city to look for her loved one. She is still feeling the intensity of this unsatisfied desire. Her soul is being torn apart. But still she has to say, at the end of verse 2, "I sought him, but I did not find him."

5. Bloch and Bloch, *Song*, 8.

In her fantasy she meets the night watchmen. At that time every city had its night watchmen. Their responsibility was to go around the city during the hours of darkness, to keep an eye open, to prevent burglaries and muggings. They were a familiar scene in those days, so not surprisingly they figure in Shulamite's imaginary expedition.

She enquires of the watchmen whether they have seen her beloved. She does not tell them his name. It does not occur to her that they will not have a clue who he is, because, as far as she is concerned, he is the only one who matters. Of course the rest of the world will be in no doubt as to his identity!

And isn't that a detail that is so true to life! How often a courting couple carry on as if there were no one else in the world. And how quick a husband and wife are to spot each other. You can pick your spouse out immediately in a crowd, because nobody else matters. This is all part of the wonderful specialness to each other of a man and a woman in love.

In verse 4, Shulamite is dreaming that the marriage arrangements are being made. The end of this waiting time is in sight, and what a relief that will be. She refers in the fourth line to the house of her mother. That phrase echoes something which is said in Genesis 24:28. Abraham has sent his servant to look for a bride for Isaac. When he meets Rebekah, she "ran and told those of her mother's house." They then arranged the marriage, and before long Rebekah was on her way to meet Isaac. The "mother's house" was a sort of slogan for the place where the marriage was arranged.

Here in verse 4 the couple are not actually married. If they had been, Shulamite would have taken Solomon to their own house. But there is some relief for the desperation of waiting love, because at least the organization of the wedding is taking place.

The presence in the inspired word of God of the theme of desperation for marriage reminds us that the passionate desire which forms part of love's craving is God-given. Married love is a gift from God to women and men. And can we not remember the feeling from our own courtship days? How tightly our heartstrings pulled! What tension we felt as we longed for the day when we could be fully united with our loved one!

Why is it that there is such a feeling of desperation in love? There are two reasons. In the first place, the one you love is so uniquely special, so indescribably beautiful, so surpassingly precious, that you are desperate for that one. And second, desperation in love is partly an expression of our awareness of the relative weakness of singleness. Right at the beginning of the Bible, God said, "It is not good that man should be alone" (Genesis 2:18); and that applies to the woman as well. God's purpose, usually, is that people should get married. On our own we are only half there. In marriage we are complete. So God has built into us these emotions that crave oneness with a husband or a wife.

That does not mean that if singleness is your calling you are not all there, or anything like that. There are some people who are given special grace from God to remain single, and special power to live as single people to his glory.

But as we read these verses, where Shulamite is remembering the tenseness of her courtship days, I think God wants those of us who are married, to be carried back in our imagination to the days of our courtship. He wants to say, do not lose the passion of those days; always feel something of this for your spouse. Cherish your spouse, show appreciation; remember how your loved one has brought satisfaction to your hungry heart, brought relief to your tortured emotions. Never lose the sense of gratitude for that. Of course, once the fulfillment of marriage comes, inevitably the pitch of emotion gets less. It would be impossible to live year after year at the height of intensity that we feel when we are courting. But nevertheless, the truths that gave rise to that depth of longing never change: you are incomplete on your own, and your beloved is incomparable. So never lose the excitement and anticipation of togetherness in love's embrace. Whenever circumstances force you to be apart for a while, be on the tenterhooks of longing for deep togetherness.

But now, remembering that the Song of Solomon shows us something of the interplay between heaven and earth, we are reminded that this feeling, this longing for love, that is part of our human make-up is a picture of something much deeper. It is a reflection at the human level of our need for God. There is something in the human heart which is desperate for union with him. The desperation for love's fulfillment which we feel within us is really a sign of our heart's hunger for God, the God who has revealed himself to us in the Lord Jesus Christ. Without him we are incomplete. Without Christ, there is an emptiness, a craving inside us. Something nags us and tells us that all is not quite right. We need God, the God who has come in the Lord Jesus to be the Savior of sinners. The challenge of these verses is that we should be determined to seek him until we find. Sin has created a vacuum inside us, but God waits to fill our lives with his love and his gracious presence.

So we may rejoice and celebrate this inner urge that drives us to seek deep satisfaction in our beloved. And may we always be able to say, My Beloved (with a capital B—my beloved Lord Jesus) is mine and I am his.

8

Be Warned!

(Song of Solomon 2:7, 15; 3:5)

We mentioned in the previous chapter that the three verses which we turn to now are warnings. The first and last ones, in chapter 2 verse 7 and chapter 3 verse 5, are identical:

> I charge you, O daughters of Jerusalem,
> By the gazelles or by the does of the field,
> Do not stir up nor awaken love
> Until it pleases.

The other word of warning, which comes in chapter 2 verse 15 is a bit different:

> Catch us the foxes,
> The little foxes that spoil the vines,
> For our vines *have* tender grapes.

All three warnings are saying basically the same thing: young people, wait for marriage. And this is a subject on which God's word is crystal clear. There is only one context where sexual experience is legitimate, and that is in the lifelong commitment in marriage of one man to one woman.

In their book on the Song of Solomon Ariel and Chana Bloch make this statement: "The biblical laws . . . are prescriptive, and they do not necessarily reflect reality."[1]

What they mean is that the Bible says that sex outside of heterosexual marriage is forbidden, but it does not follow that sexual temptation was unknown in Jewish society, nor that sexual purity was invariably maintained there. Amongst the Jews, as anywhere else, young people might be tempted to sin in this area. Premarital sex and promiscuity were as much a danger there as in any Gentile community. So this warning was, and is, necessary.

And in the day and age in which we live it is certainly as necessary as ever. We live at a time when sex outside of marriage is regarded as perfectly normal, and when marriage itself is corrupted by redefinitions which cause total confusion as to what marriage actually is. So we have the false concept of gay marriage paraded before us constantly. We hear repeatedly the lie that homosexuality is quite normal and fully acceptable for some people. We are invited to live in a world of make-believe, where gender identity is supposed to be fluid and open to personal choice. We have legislation passed to make divorce easy, and we hear that awful word "partner" constantly.

And in such a context, the obligation is laid upon us to stress, unashamedly, the biblical teaching that the only valid definition of marriage is that it is between one man and one woman exclusively, and that it lasts for life. To insist that this is so is part of the way that we fulfil our duty to love our neighbor, as we reach out to those deluded by sin, praying that they may be rescued from that "way that seems right to a man, but its end is the way of death" (Proverbs 14:12 and 16:25).

Moreover, stressing the biblical morality at this point in time, at this stage in the development of western culture, is vitally necessary in order to protect our young people growing up in an environment so riddled with temptation, as well as to undergird for all of us the commitment to marital faithfulness in a society where adultery is no longer frowned upon, and also to prevent any of us

1. Bloch and Bloch, *Song*, 14.

from being sucked into a warped view of married life and love. The need to stand out as different, as a holy people, a people separated in Christ from a godless world in this respect, is one of the pressing needs of our time. I am reminded in this connection of something which a lady called Elizabeth Rundle Charles wrote back in 1864, having been influenced by reading the works of Martin Luther:

> If I profess with loudest voice and clearest exposition every portion of the truth of God except that little point which the world and the Devil are at that moment attacking, I am not confessing Christ, however boldly I may be professing Christ. Where the battle rages, there the loyalty of the soldier is proved, and to be steady on all the battlefield besides, is mere flight and disgrace if he flinches at that point.[2]

And in his wisdom, the Holy Spirit has inspired these warnings to be written into the word of God here in the Song of Solomon.

As we have noted, the words of the first and last warnings are exactly the same. But although that is so, the setting is different in each case. In 2:7 it follows a passage, stretching back to 1:9, where, as we saw earlier, the couple sing together of married life as they have enjoyed it as a married couple. By contrast, the repeat of the warning in 3:5 comes, as we saw in the last chapter, at the end of one of the flashback passages, a section which looks back to courtship days before the couple are married.

In both cases Shulamite is speaking. She is addressing, once again, those "daughters of Jerusalem," that anonymous group of young ladies, standing for young, single women in general. She is warning them to avoid sexual sin. The warning message of these two verses may be summed up like this:

YOUNG LADIES, WAIT FOR MARRIAGE.

In the first instance Shulamite speaks out of her own experience of having kept herself for her husband. Now, having been married for some time, she can see that waiting for the wedding has made for a

2. Charles, *Chronicles*, loc. 3838.

wonderful marriage. She is telling from personal experience what heights of pleasure there are in married love if you keep yourself for your husband, if you resist every temptation to engage in premarital affairs. She speaks with happy hindsight. She has proved it from her own experience of having waited.

And now Shulamite wants to help young women who are not yet married to avoid falling into the trap of seeking sexual pleasure prematurely. The warning amounts to the advice: you young ladies, wait for marriage. Shulamite is reminding all girls, that there is a proper time for the ripening of sexual desire. God's command is, keep yourself for your husband. So you must avoid putting yourself in a risky situation before you are married. There is something so wonderfully sacred about sexual love in its proper context: we speak, do we not, of the sanctity of marriage. So a solemn charge against the danger of premarital sex is necessary.

When the warning is repeated in 3:5, it is set, as we have said, in a different context. The words now come after a passage in which Shulamite, as a single woman, anticipates her wedding. She is desperate as she waits to be married to her beloved. In this new context the warning recognizes that the temptation to engage in sexual activity outside of marriage can be very strong. The relief of this desperate desire seems so good. To be released from emotional tension appears to be a very desirable thing. But here is a young girl, not yet married in this context, speaking to others who are in the same position as she is. She too, like them, longs for love's completion. She craves the pleasure which comes from the embrace of a lover. But she shows wisdom. She realizes that premature lovemaking will ruin everything.

There are some people today, just as there were some in those days, who say, if you are so desperate, who cares? What can be wrong if consenting adults do it in private? But we have to remember that the Song of Solomon comes from the section of the Old Testament known as the Wisdom Literature. It shows us the true perspective on things as defined by the one who is (and I am using the Authorized Version just now) "the only wise God," words found three times in the New Testament (Romans 16:27, 1 Timothy 1:17, and Jude 25). And surely if the Bible stresses exactly the same point three times, it makes it very emphatic indeed. God is the only source of true wisdom, and we must heed his instructions. He alone, through his word, offers us real wisdom as to how to live. And the Old Testament Wisdom Literature points us to how real human wisdom must be defined.

The fact is that premature lovemaking is actually sinful human foolishness. There is no wisdom in it at all. It just brings you down to the depths of ruin and misery. So wise Shulamite says to young girls like herself, beware of that danger; wait for the right time.

The reference to the gazelle and the doe is illuminated by Deuteronomy 12:22, which says, "the gazelle and the deer are eaten" (and anyone who is familiar with *The Sound of Music* will know that a doe is "a deer, a female deer"). By referring to the gazelle and the doe, or the deer, Shulamite is facing the fact that premature sexual activity eats you, it devours your personality and your character. It eats up the life of a girl. It does not please, she implies: it is too soon; there is no pleasure in it. People think there is. It may bring a pleasant sensation momentarily, but there is no true pleasure, no lasting pleasure. In the long run it brings great grief and heartache, a bitter fruit to swallow afterwards. So "do not stir up nor awaken love until it pleases," otherwise you will have to live with lasting, debilitating displeasure. So, she says, young ladies, wait for marriage.

But we turn now to the other warning (2:15). This time it is addressed to young men. And the warning can be summarized in parallel with the previous one, like this:

YOUNG MEN, WAIT FOR MARRIAGE.

Although it is not made clear whose words these are, it seems probable that Solomon is speaking. He is passing on the same warning against premarital sex to young men that Shulamite has passed on to young ladies. Young men are not to defile the dignity of women through promiscuity.

The way in which he words his warning may well make its relevance to such a subject seem rather obscure. But there are three other biblical references to foxes that help us to understand what this warning is getting at.

In Ezekiel 13:4 the Lord says: "O Israel, your prophets are like foxes in the deserts." In verse 2 he has described them as prophets "who prophesy out of their own heart," and in verse 3 he has called them "foolish prophets." Then in verse 6 he says that "they have envisioned futility." And that is the key word here. These supposed prophets who are not actually proclaiming the Lord's word are doing something futile, something pointless, worthless. They are liars. And if a young man pressurizes his girlfriend into having premarital sex, then he is like a deceptive fox. He is perpetrating something that, in the end will prove to be utterly empty and frustrating, and will bring immense disappointment to his young lady friend.

Then Lamentations 5:18 refers to "Mount Zion which is desolate, with foxes walking about on it." This desolation is explained by several terms in the preceding verses. The chapter begins by mentioning "our reproach" in verse 1. Verse 5 says that we "have no rest." In verse 15 the lament is worded, "the joy of our heart has ceased; our dance has turned into mourning." In verse 11 the people of Jerusalem have to mourn the fact that their enemies "ravished the women in Zion," and then, in verse 16, they have to face up to the fact that "we have sinned." In the same way a young man who leads his young lady into sin will cause her to have a restless heart, a feeling of utter joylessness. He will bring her into a sense of self-reproach. It must not be done, says Solomon.

And then in Luke 13:32, when Jesus is informed by some Pharisees that Herod wants to kill him, he responds by describing Herod as "that fox." William Hendriksen suggests that Jesus used this term because of Herod's "slyness or craftiness."[3] Burrowes speaks of "stealth and cunning."[4] The fox is known as a stealthy and crafty creature. And there is something sly and cunning about the young man who wants to pressurize his girlfriend into premature lovemaking.

---

3. Hendriksen, *Luke*, 709.
4. Burrowes, *Song*, 237.

In our verse here in Song of Solomon 2:15 foxes are said to "spoil the vines." A sexually promiscuous young man is a spoiler. He spoils womanhood in general, because he conveys a false impression of what women are, and what women are for. He spoils that particular girl's psychological well-being. He spoils his own marriage when it comes later. He spoils his own character, defiling himself, and undermining his own strength of personality. He spoils love. He spoils family life. He spoils society, because married love is the basic building block of society.

As is true in several contexts in the Song of Solomon, so here the vine represents femininity. Vines, we read "have tender grapes." There is something tender about femininity. Women must not be abused. It is irresponsibility on the part of a man to sleep with a woman to whom he is not married.

So Solomon says, "catch us the foxes." Because it does nothing but spoil, the fox is fit only to be caught and despatched.

So taken together the three warnings in these verses add up to this: whoever you are, wait for marriage before starting to indulge your sexual appetite.

And to be crystal clear on this matter is a vital part of godly living, an essential part of Christian witness, in the world of today.

But there is one thing which we must emphasize very strongly, and that is that sexual sin is not the unforgiveable sin. We may need to explain very clearly and directly, without any hesitancy, to people today what God has to say on these matters. But that is, primarily, so that no one caves in to despair. Fanny Crosby put it brilliantly:

> The vilest offender who truly believes
> That moment from Jesus a pardon receives.[5]

It is a marvellous statement that we read in 1 Corinthians 6:9–11:

> Do you not know that the unrighteous will not inherit the kingdom of God? Do not be deceived. Neither fornicators, nor idolaters, nor adulterers, nor homosexuals, nor sodomites, nor thieves, nor covetous, nor drunkards,

---

5. From the hymn, *To God be the glory*, Fanny J. Crosby (1820–1915).

> nor revilers, nor extortioners will inherit the kingdom of
> God. And such were some of you. But you were washed,
> but you were sanctified, but you were justified in the
> name of the Lord Jesus and by the Spirit of our God.

In the church there at Corinth there were believers who had
been saved out of a background of sexual sins of every conceiv-
able kind. Some had committed fornication. They were the young
men and women that the Song of Solomon was addressing in these
warnings, who had anticipated the wedding day, and in some cases,
perhaps, had engaged in promiscuous relationships with more than
one partner. Some had been guilty of adultery. Some had fallen
victim to homosexual pressure. In those days, in the Roman Em-
pire, homosexual sin was as trendy as it seems to be today. Others had been "sodomites." F. F. Bruce suggests, probably correctly,
that the words "homosexual" and "sodomite" refer respectively to
the female and male roles in a homosexual relationship.[6] Another
equivalent today of the former would be the man who undergoes
what gets called "gender transitioning" and tries to present himself
as if he were female.

But now the apostle, inspired by the Spirit of God, can rejoice
that "such *were* some of you." In other words, you are not any more.
You have been forgiven by the grace of the Lord Jesus. You have
been transformed by the power of the Spirit of the Lord Jesus. After
living a life of abnormality in sin, you have been restored to what
human life is supposed to be as created by God. And that change
is vital. Paul makes no allowance for someone who says that they
have been converted but just goes on living in his old sinful ways.
The compelling and indispensable evidence of a sound conversion
to Christ is that sin is rejected, repented of, and a new life of obe-
dience begins in which there is no place for fornication, adultery,
homosexuality, or tampering with one's God-given gender.

I was reading the other day the report of an interview with a
man who had been involved in homosexuality but had then been
converted. The interviewer asked him whether he thought there
could be such a thing as a gay Christian. His reply was, "they are

6. Bruce, *Corinthians*, 61.

totally irreconcilable." He said that such a phrase is as nonsensical as to describe yourself as a greedy Christian. And neither is there any sense in terms such as "a Christian living with a partner," or "a Christian adulterer." Yes, all sin must be broken with if our profession of faith in Christ is genuine, but no sin is an insurmountable obstacle to God's forgiving mercy.

And to say "all sin must be broken with" ensures that not one of us can ever sit back smugly and say, well at least I haven't committed any of those sins we've just been talking about. Just glance at two of the other sins in Paul's list in that passage from 1 Corinthians 6.

He mentions covetousness. That is dissatisfaction with what you have got and the longing for more of this world's material goods. There were some of those Corinthian Christians who used to be guilty of that sin, and for that reason were numbered amongst "the unrighteous [who] will not inherit the kingdom of God." But they too have been changed. They discarded covetousness and now live in thorough contentment with God's provision.

Then there were some in the church at Corinth who had been revilers. That is the sort of person who is very quick to react, to voice his own opinion, especially about other people, someone who does not care if he wounds the feelings of a sensitive soul, but who is constantly criticising those he disagrees with. That sort of person is not en route to heaven, Paul says. But he can rejoice that those of the Corinthian Christians who used to be like that have been changed by the power of Christ, and their destiny has been totally reversed.

Now I draw our attention to those two sins from Paul's list in particular, because perhaps they are the ones that any of us might be most prone to. Notice that they are in the very same list as those awful sexual sins, because in God's sight they are just as awful. And if we have been forgiven and enabled to repent and gain victory over our sins, then there is nothing to prevent God from achieving the same victory in the life of a homosexual, a transgender victim, a promiscuous teenager, or whomever.

And we need to add this comment: that repentance is not an all at once and once for all event. We have to go on battling against sin, repenting of sin, for as long as we live. And if we are tempted to develop a covetous spirit yet again, even after we have been forgiven, we should not be surprised if someone from a promiscuous background, or someone converted out of homosexuality, goes on facing the same temptations, and having to renew repentance, and seek daily grace for ongoing victory. And the glorious thing is that we are not just left to achieve this in our own strength. We have God's almighty resources to enable us to overcome again and again. And that is the wonderful power of the gospel.

But there is one other thing that we must consider before we finish with these warning verses. If part of the purpose of the Song of Solomon is to raise our sights to the heavenly love of Jesus Christ for his church, how do these verses fit into that theme?

Perhaps the answer is that we are being challenged to respond to that heavenly love with faithfulness. To become a Christian is to be wedded to Christ in an exclusive relationship. In 2 Corinthians 11:2, the apostle Paul says this: "I am jealous for you with godly jealousy. For I have betrothed you to one husband, that I may present you as a chaste virgin to Christ." He goes on to explain that our spiritual chastity would be compromised if we were to receive a different gospel, a gospel which really preached an alternative Jesus. This would result in our minds being "corrupted from the simplicity that is in Christ," as verse 3 puts it.

The word "simplicity" here speaks of single-minded devotedness, loyalty without mixed motives. It is the opposite of trying to interweave dual loyalties which really conflict with each other. The alternative gospel which Paul dreaded was one which offered the opportunity of having a foot in both camps. It would allow people to follow Christ up to a point, while also pursuing worldly ambitions, and courting popularity in a godless society.

Jesus used a very similar word when he said in Luke 11:34, "The lamp of the body is the eye. Therefore, when your eye is good, your whole body also is full of light. But when your eye is bad, your body also is full of darkness." The word translated "good" is related to the word for "simplicity" in the 2 Corinthians passage. The Authorized Version actually uses the word "single" there in Jesus' statement; it reads: "when thine eye is single, thy whole body also is full of light." What the Lord is saying is that a good eye is one that sees clearly because it is looking in just one direction. A bad eye, is one that is looking one way while trying to glance the other as well. The result is that nothing is clear. Your surroundings might as well be pitch black. You are living in the dark. But if your eye is good your attention is riveted on a single thing, and that is an enlightening state of affairs. So he is calling us to look with a single eye in his direction, and to shut out of our minds, to block out of our attention, the attractions of this sinful world.

This exclusive, unadulterated devotion to the Lord is what the apostle John is getting at when he says: "Do not love the world or the things in the world. If anyone loves the world, the love of the Father is not in him" (1 John 2:15). Jesus makes the same point in a slightly different way: "No one can serve two masters; for either he will hate the one and love the other, or else he will be loyal to the one and despise the other. You cannot serve God and mammon" (Matthew 6:24). I reckon we could omit that last word and still capture what Jesus was really getting at: "you cannot serve God and . . . ." You cannot serve God and anything else. Genuine service of God flows out of an exclusive love for Jesus. James, in fact, compares love for the world with adultery: "Adulterers and adulteresses! Do you not know that friendship with the world is enmity with God?" (James 4:4). As Jesus said in Mark 12:30: "you shall love the Lord your God with *all* your heart, with *all* your soul, with *all* your mind, and with *all* your strength."

9

Wedding Bells

(Song of Solomon 3:6–11)

Yes, wedding bells are sounding as we reach this next section of the Song of Solomon. Here we have the wedding scene. We must remember that the Song is not a chronological account of the love of this couple. It jumps backwards and forwards. It is looking at love from different angles. So here right in the middle of the book the wedding is taking place. The couple were married at the beginning of the book. They were courting at the beginning of this chapter. And now there's the wedding. The Song is bringing different aspects from here and there to show what a wonderful thing love is in the context of marriage.

We have described the opening verses of this chapter as an account of the sense of desperation that a courting couple may feel as they wait for marriage. Well, for all the frustrations of the waiting time, it does come to an end at last, and these verses celebrate the glad relief of a satisfied love.

This whole section is building up to the climax of the final line. The wedding day is a day of gladness. Especially is that true for the happy couple, specifically in verse 11 for Solomon, but surely for Shulamite too, as she becomes his wife. The desperate period of waiting is over. The months of anticipation have come to an end. The day of fulfilment and satisfaction has arrived. They are united as husband and wife. They are free now to enjoy what they have been desperately waiting for. The result is relief and gladness.

I commented previously that I have come to the conclusion that, apart from four places, there are only two characters who speak in this Song, Shulamite and Solomon. This is the first of those four passages where I think we do hear other voices. It seems that this section represents the excited and admiring voices of the wedding guests.

These verses are a single section to do with the wedding day, but they fall into two subsections, verse 6 stands alone, and then verses 7–11 belong together.

Verse 6 asks a question, but the following verses must not be read as the answer to the question. It is actually a rhetorical question. No answer is given, because the answer is so blatantly obvious—at least it was to the people who originally voiced the question, even if it is perhaps not immediately clear to us reading it today.

The opening words of the question, "Who is this coming out of the wilderness . . . ?" are repeated almost exactly in chapter 8 verse 5, which reads, "who is this coming up from the wilderness," followed by the words, "leaning upon her beloved?" That final comment makes it obvious who "this" is: it is the bride; it is Shulamite. So chapter 3 verse 6 is about her. What we have here is an exalted description of the bride's triumphant splendor on her wedding day. We might say that verse 6 is the ancient equivalent of that modern ditty which has been set to *The Bridal Chorus* from Wagner's *Lohengrin*, "Here comes the bride."

The second line of the verse echoes Joel 2:30, which also refers to pillars of smoke. It reads like this: "I will show wonders in the heavens and in the earth: blood and fire and pillars of smoke." Joel is talking about the wonders that God will do in the end times. One of those wonders is portrayed in terms of pillars of smoke. And here the bride is being compared to pillars of smoke. In other words, when you see this beautiful bride, you are looking at a true wonder, a woman resplendent in her feminine beauty. And that beauty is focused, as the rest of the verse indicates, in the sweet fragrance of her perfumes.

In Solomon's day, merchant traders brought in massive wealth to the kingdom. We read about it in 1 Kings 10:14–15: "The weight of gold that came to Solomon yearly was six hundred and sixty-six talents of gold, besides that from the travelling merchants, from the income of traders." In the world of those days, trading in aromatic spices was a very important part of the international economy. We get a clue to that from Ezekiel 27:22: "The merchants of Sheba and Raamah were your merchants. They traded for your wares the choicest spices." This description of the wealth that the merchants bring is telling us that in the approach of the bride we are catching a glimpse of something that money just cannot buy, something far more valuable than all the wealth of the merchants put together. Here is a woman, no mere commodity, but someone precious, special, unique, fragrant with all the merchants' spices at once. Gold and silver are nothing in comparison with a bride. The bridegroom is waiting for a treasure the like of which he has never handled before.

Those of us who are husbands must remember our wedding day. How regal your wife looked then. She was so stunning in her beauty, dressed up just for you. Didn't you feel, what a treasure! I hope that you have never stopped feeling that. I hope that the day of gladness was just the doorway into a life of gladness in enjoyment of your wife. We are to find lifelong gladness in our wives and treat them as a priceless jewel.

In verses 7–11 the attention shifts to the bridegroom. We are still hearing the voices of the wedding guests. Their starting-point in this passage is to observe that Solomon is being carried in his couch. Verses 9 and 10 give us a fuller description of that couch: it is a palanquin, that is to say, a sedan chair, and Solomon is being carried in it to his wedding.

But this is no ordinary sedan chair. It is an exceptionally splendid sedan chair. Sedan chairs were first introduced in the UK in 1634 as a means of public transport. They became very popular very quickly. A sedan chair was carried on poles by two men, one at each end. They were cheaper to hire than a carriage, and could often get you to places faster, because they could fit down streets that were too narrow for a carriage. Because they could sway and bounce as the men tried to get you to your destination in the quickest possible time, they were not recommended if you suffered from motion sickness. Very soon, rather more deluxe sedan chairs became popular amongst the wealthy gentry. A wealthy family would own their own sedan chair. It would be kept in the hall, and would be finely decorated to match the décor of the house.[1]

Well it was one of those posher types of sedan chair that Solomon was using. We learn that it was made of the choicest materials. Cedar wood, silver, gold, and cloth made from royal purple, are all mentioned in verses 9 and 10. Verse 10 informs us that it was the pillars that were silver. The word "pillars" is an interesting one. It can either mean the massive pillars that hold up a huge building, or it can mean something more like a tent pole. We have an example of the former use in 1 Kings 7, and of the latter in Exodus 27.

1 Kings 7:2–3 tells us that Solomon "built the House of the Forest of Lebanon; its length was one hundred cubits [that is about 50 yards or 46 meters], its width fifty cubits [25 yards, 23 meters], and its height thirty cubits [15 yards or 14 meters], with four rows of cedar pillars, and cedar beams on the pillars. And it was panelled with cedar above the beams that were on forty-five pillars, fifteen to a row." So those were massive pillars made from cedar wood.

Then Exodus 27:10 is talking about the tabernacle in the wilderness. It gives the instruction that "its twenty pillars and their twenty sockets shall be bronze." The pillars needed for a tent would be much narrower than those needed for a massive house. And here in Song of Solomon 3:10 it is this thin type of pole that is in view. There was one at each of the four corners of the sedan chair, and they held up the roof.

The last two lines of verse 10, "its interior paved with love by the daughters of Jerusalem," probably mean that some of Solomon's artistic young female servants have decorated the inside with love scenes appropriate for the wedding day.

---

1. Castelow, *Sedan Chair*, paras. 2–4, 9.

Glancing back at verses 7–8, we have a description of the splendor of Solomon's retinue. All his bodyguards have turned out. There are sixty of them. They are dressed in their official regalia with their swords. They do not need to use them today, but they are dressed up for the occasion. Their normal task is to provide protection for the king at night, as the end of verse 8 says. But today they have a happier responsibility. They form an escort for the king as he comes to claim his bride.

When we get to verse 11 we reach the climax of this vivid portrait of Solomon's splendor on his wedding day. We now discover the main purpose of this elaborate description of the bride in verse 6 and the bridegroom in verses 7–10. It is "the day of the gladness of his heart." The whole passage has been intended to convey this atmosphere of joy that pervades the wedding day, the joy of fulfilment. The desperation of love's waiting time is over. There is glad relief as love is satisfied in the marriage union. But this is only the beginning of a lifetime of love with all its pleasures.

Apparently, it was customary in Jewish weddings to place crowns on the heads of the bride and bridegroom. That is what verse 11 is referring to. This would not have been the crown of gold borrowed from the royal treasury, the crown that the king would wear on ceremonial occasions. The wedding crown used to be a wreath made of leaves and twigs. And it was understood as a symbol of happiness.

So as we who are married recall the glad relief that we felt on our wedding day, the day when the desperation of waiting came to an end, the day when love's satisfaction became our joy, then the Song of Solomon is inviting us to celebrate. The Song is above everything else a celebration of married love. And we celebrate by giving thanks to God the Creator for this amazing pleasure which he has put into our human nature. We celebrate by expressing thanks constantly to our wife, our husband, for the gladness of heart that she, that he, has brought us over the years and brings us still to this day. We celebrate too by redoubling our own efforts to make our spouse's life one of continuing gladness and joy.

But now the time has come again to lift our sights, to remind ourselves just how much God enjoys his people. The Lord Jesus

Christ enjoys his bride, the church. Just as the wedding guests can identify with Solomon's appreciation of his fragrant bride in all her beautiful splendor, so our Savior revels in the attractiveness to him of his people.

In Psalm 45:13–15 we find a passage which has a close resemblance to verse 6 of our chapter here: "The royal daughter is all glorious within the palace; her clothing is woven with gold. She shall be brought to the King in robes of many colors; the virgins, her companions who follow her, shall be brought to you. With gladness and rejoicing they shall be brought; they shall enter the King's palace."

Richard Belcher rightly reads Psalm 45 as portraying a royal wedding "as a type of the relationship between Christ the king and his bride, the church." In these verses, 13–15, the bride is "brought to the king in all her beauty with her attendants." Belcher then makes a cross reference to Revelation 19:6–8. That passage reads as follows:

> I heard, as it were, the voice of a great multitude, as the sound of many waters and as the sound of mighty thunderings, saying, "Alleluia! For the Lord God Omnipotent reigns! Let us be glad and rejoice and give him glory, for the marriage of the Lamb has come, and his wife has made herself ready." And to her it was granted to be arrayed in fine linen, clean and bright, for the fine linen is the righteous acts of the saints.

Belcher observes that here the bride of Christ "is presented clothed with linen bright and pure, symbolic of the righteous deeds of the saints." He notes that that passage "especially emphasizes the multitude of guests and the great joy of the occasion," and comments that "the coming of the king . . . generates tremendous joy and celebration."[2]

Yes, indeed, there is a day coming when the bride of Christ, that is to say, all believing people throughout the world, will enjoy the glad relief of final union with their beloved Savior in heaven. For now, we still wait with desperate longing, but what bliss there

---

2. Belcher, *Messiah and Psalms*, 129–30, 133–4.

will be on the day when that longing is fulfilled, when faith turns to sight at the appearing of the Lord. That will be joy forever. And it is a wonderful reflection of that heavenly union which is found in the earthly union of man and wife.

10

The Husband's Admiration for his Wife

(Song of Solomon 4:1–15)

The main theme running through this entire passage is the husband's admiration for his wife. But we may subdivide the passage into two parts, and we start by focussing on verses 1–7. We can identify these verses as dealing with a single theme because of the repetition in verse 7 of the sentiment of the first verse. In verse 1 Solomon says, "Behold, you are fair, my love! Behold, you are fair!" And then in verse 7 he repeats, "You are all fair, my love." That repetition holds these verses together as a coherent section:

ALL FAIR

As we are continually seeing in these studies, a major reason why God created man in his own image, male and female, was so that a man and a woman may find pleasure in each other. God invented marriage so that one man and one woman could discover the possibility of pleasure escalating as they enjoy each other over the course of a lifetime.

Ecclesiastes 9:9 says: "Live joyfully with the wife whom you love all the days of your vain life which he has given you under the sun, all your days of vanity; for that is your portion in life, and in the labor which you perform under the sun."

We live in a world of vanity and labor because of the damage done by sin. However, there is one bright spot where it is possible to capture again something of the glory and splendor, something of the genuine pleasure, from which we have fallen, and that is in the joy of married love.

The psychologist, Arnold Buss writes, "Pleasure is available through all the senses," and then goes on to describe how pleasure may be stimulated by the sight of a beautiful scene, by the taste of delicious food, by the sweet scent of perfume, by the sound of rhythmic or melodious music, or by touch, whether it be "the soft touch of fur," or "the rough feeling of a massage."[1] In this passage we discover how all of our God-given senses come into play in the experience of love between husband and wife. The husband is voicing his admiration for his wife, prompted by her appeal to his various senses.

Throughout these verses the wife's beauty is being described. Solomon is exclaiming that his wife is exquisitely beautiful, staggeringly attractive. His adulation reaches its summit in those words in verse 7, where he says, "you are all fair." All of her, every inch of her body, every aspect of her being, every facet of her character, is beautiful in the eyes of her husband.

Notice that all five senses come into play.

Sight

Solomon is looking at his wife. First, in verse 1, he looks at her eyes and her hair. Her eyes are so picturesque, as beautiful as a dove's eyes. Her hair is thick and wavy, so much so that it reminds him of looking from a distance at a mountain side where there is a flock of goats descending the hill. The movement of the goats seems to

1. Buss, *Psychology*, 147.

make the whole hillside come to life. This is a way of expressing the luscious beauty of his wife's appearance.

Then, in verses 2 and 3, he looks a little lower, at her teeth and her lips. Her teeth remind him of "shorn sheep which have come up from the washing." If you go out into the fields after a wet spell, how brown the sheep can look! Their wool is spattered with mud. But go when they have been shorn and dipped. How brightly they stand out against the green of the pastures then. The wife's teeth are brilliant white. They are in pairs. That is the significance of the reference to twins in verse 2. There are no ugly gaps. There is one above and one below all the way round her mouth—perfect symmetry. The husband admires God's design which he sees in his wife, and the lips in front of the teeth are just as admirable as the teeth themselves.

Next, in verse 4, he moves his eyes down a little more. He finds the sight of her neck just as enticing. She is a woman of poise and gracefulness. The imagery in verse 4 draws on a custom of those days. When armies were not out at war they used to hang up their shields on the walls of their city. As Ezekiel notes, this custom created an impression of splendor and perfect beauty. Here is what he says in chapter 27 verses 10 and 11:

> Those from Persia, Lydia, and Libya were in your army as men of war; they hung shield and helmet in you; they gave splendor to you. Men of Arvad with your army were on your walls all around, and the men of Gammad were in your towers; they hung their shields on your walls all around; they made your beauty perfect.

Just as perfect and splendid is the wife's beauty. As the husband looks at his wife, she stimulates his sense of sight. He admires the beauty he can see.

Sound

In the second line of verse 3 the husband finds the wife's mouth lovely. This is probably a reference to the words which come from her mouth. It is not just the sight of her lips which is so admirable.

The sound of her voice also captivates her husband's admiration. It is so delightful to hear her speak. So he admires the beauty he can hear.

Touch

The last two lines of verse 3 compare the wife's temples to a pomegranate, a fruit with a very smooth, curved skin. We are to imagine the husband gently stroking his wife's face. It is so pleasantly soft. It feels delectable. He is admiring the beauty he can touch.

Taste

We have commented before that the thing about fawns and gazelles, mentioned in verse 5, is that they were eaten. Four times in Deuteronomy regulations are given about the eating of these particular animals. Here is just one example, from Deuteronomy 14:4–5: "These are the animals which you may eat: the ox, the sheep, the goat, the deer, the gazelle, the roe deer," and one or two others.[2]

According to 1 Kings 4:22–23, in Solomon's own time gazelle meat was part of the daily provision in the king's household. Those verses read like this: "Now Solomon's provision for one day was thirty kors of fine flour, sixty kors of meal, ten fatted oxen, twenty oxen from the pastures, and one hundred sheep, besides deer, gazelles, roebucks, and fatted fowl." Gazelle meat was a regular food, and no doubt had a very enjoyable taste.

Here the husband is in effect saying to his wife, you are so delightfully tasty, I could eat you! And so he admires the beauty he can almost taste.

Smell

Verse 6 speaks of the mountain of myrrh and the hill of frankincense. Myrrh and frankincense were fragrant spices. Back in 2:17 the wife invited her husband to express his love to her in similar

---

2. See also Deut. 12:15, 22; 15:22.

words. She wanted them to be together day and night. Here the husband responds to her invitation. He says, I am going to love you from now until daybreak. The myrrh and frankincense of her perfume are so exotic, so pleasing. All night and all day he will revel in the sweetness of her scent. He admires the beauty he can smell.

And then the last line of verse 7 sums it all up. Whether the husband contemplates his wife's appearance, or the sound of her voice, the feel of her skin, her imaginary taste, or the fragrance of her scent, everything is just the epitome of perfection. She is spotlessly attractive. Every sense has been stimulated to prompt him to admire her beauty.

The challenge of these verses is that this is how every husband should regard his wife, and these are the kind of things that he should tell her. Those of us who are husbands must face this challenge. Do I admire my wife? Is my admiration as strong now as ever it was? Am I enjoying the stimulation of every sense—and telling my wife how much I adore her? Have I got as much imagination as Solomon had to find words to express my love? We may need to find different imagery these days. A modern wife might not take kindly to being described as a tower or a pomegranate. But there are other images which are just as appropriate today as those were back then. We must let the words of praise to our wives flow freely with all the imagination we can muster, as we express our sincere admiration.

And now, once again, the love portrayed in the Song of Solomon points us upwards to that higher, greater love, the love of Christ for the church and for each Christian as an individual. Psalm 50:2 tells us that the Lord sees Zion (a symbol of the church) as "the perfection of beauty." That is how much he loves us. We are aware so often of our own ugliness because of sin. But our Savior's love transforms us. It transforms God's view of us. In Christ God sees us as spotless, without blemish. He enjoys us, and we may enjoy him. Psalm 33 begins with these words: "Rejoice in the Lord, O you righteous! For praise from the upright is beautiful." Just as Solomon admired the beauty of Shulamite's voice, so the Lord truly appreciates hearing the praise of his people. The sound of our voices raised in hymns of praise is genuinely enticing to him. And when we think how raucous our singing must really be, it is, as always, only because of his astonishing grace that the Lord finds us so attractive. And so we praise him yet again, and rest in the assurance of his love for us.

The theme of the husband's admiration for his wife continues as we move on to verses 8–15. We have an indication that this is a complete section by the repetition of the word "Lebanon" in the first line of verse 8 and the last line of verse 15. This word brackets these verses together, and the controlling theme is:

TIME AND SPACE FOR ENJOYMENT

The husband is still speaking, but the section is in two main parts which overlap each other. In verses 8–12, every verse contains the word "spouse." That fact signals that those verses form a subsection. But if we start again at verse 12 and go through to verse 15 we find the imagery of a garden. Both the first and last of these verses refer to gardens and to fountains. Verse 12 comes in both subsections and forms a sort of bridge between them. This means that we can actually divide this section into three.

First, we have, in 4:8–11, an invitation issued by the husband to his wife, in which he anticipates what we might call

The Depths and Heights of Love's Enjoyment

The passage begins with the invitation, "Come with me." The husband is inviting his wife into the depths of seclusion that love always demands, there to experience the heights of joy that love brings.

As he begins to speak the couple are in Lebanon—not literally, but in his imagination. The mountains of Lebanon were famous for their deep, secluded valleys, and Solomon is saying, let's imagine ourselves in such a situation where we'll be undisturbed in our togetherness, where nobody else will find us; let's have time and space to enjoy each other.

But then the scene changes. Opposite the mountains of Lebanon there is another range of mountains, which included Amana, Senir and Hermon. Senir and Hermon are actually two names for the same mountain in different languages. It was the highest mountain in this range. So now Solomon is saying, we've gone down deep in our emotions into the valley of love's seclusion; let's also scale the heights in our love for each other. The enjoyment of husband and wife in married love is both deep experience, and a sense of rising high above everything.

The New American Standard Bible paraphrases the reference to the ravished heart in verse 9 with the words, "You have made my heart beat faster." One commentator renders it, "You leave me breathless."[3] That is the joyful depth and height, the excitement of love.

In verse 10 we hear an echo of the very first words of the book after the title. In 1:2–3 the wife spoke of her husband's love being better than wine and preferable to any perfume. Now he is saying the same to her. As far as he is concerned, the sweet scent that his wife exudes is far to be preferred to the most costly, exotic, perfumed spices which can be imported from the farthest part of the world. He is so enraptured with her. They are caught up together in the joy of each other. Nothing in all the world is more exotic to a husband than his wife. In verse 11 the depths and heights of emotion lead to the sweet sensation of honey as the couple kiss each other.

As we have said, the Song of Solomon is before anything else a celebration of married love, and an invitation to join the celebration. So we give thanks to God who created the joys of married love. And the celebration brings with it a challenge not to lose our joy, to let our imagination run riot in expressing the enjoyment we find in our spouse. As Solomon knew, we need to create time and space to be undisturbed in seclusion, to be alone together, to develop our relationship and rise to the heights in our enjoyment of each other.

But now we must remember that the same kind of joy is found in the love between the Christian and the Savior, and we celebrate that as well. How wonderful that the Lord Jesus can express these same sentiments as he contemplates us. He finds us ravishing—how remarkable! He actually appreciates being loved by us. We are reminded here of the importance of love's seclusion: if our relationship

3. Garrett, *Song*, 185.

with the Lord is to go deep, each of us needs those times that we spend entirely alone with him. Only as we go deep with him in prayer and in his word will we rise to the heights of joy in his grace.

But now let's look at that bridging verse, 4:12. The emphasis now is on:

The Exclusiveness of True Love

As we saw when we were considering those warning verses from chapters 2 and 3, the Song of Solomon is totally opposed to all forms of sexual activity outside marriage. That is a tragic travesty of what God created to be enjoyed. It is a mere mockery of God's creation gift, and is an insult to the Creator himself. It demands repentance. This verse is another warning of the destructive evil of lovemaking without marriage.

The wife is described as "a garden enclosed"—a walled garden with a locked gate—and as "a spring shut up, a fountain sealed"—a private water supply which is sealed off from the general public. She is not shut up from her husband, but shut up for him alone. The wife and the husband belong exclusively to each other. To everyone else in the world she is enclosed, shut up, sealed. Marriage is a private sphere which is impenetrable to outsiders.

Notice that in this verse, as also in verses 9 and 10, the husband refers to his wife as "my sister, my spouse." That is an important phrase. It does not of course mean that Shulamite was Solomon's biological sister. That was not the case at all. But it does remind us that marriage must take place within the brotherhood and sisterhood of the faith. In the days of Ezra and Nehemiah some of the Israelites had married foreign women who had not come to share their faith in the one Lord God. Ezra had to rebuke the people in these words: "You have transgressed and have taken pagan wives, adding to the guilt of Israel" (Ezra 10:10). The New Testament instruction reads like this: "Do not be unequally yoked together with unbelievers. For what fellowship has righteousness with lawlessness? And what communion has light with darkness?" (2 Corinthians 6:14). That verse is not referring only to marriage, but marriage is one valid application of the principle. In the case of a Christian widow, the same principle applies: "she is at liberty to be married to whom she wishes, only in the Lord" (1 Corinthians 7:39). This is an important biblical command, which we must be unashamed to assert. It seems, as a matter of observation, that, when a believer foolishly marries an unbeliever, it is more often the believer whose faith suffers, not the unbeliever who is won for Christ. There are happy and gracious exceptions, but God's word is clear on our duty.

And, of course, behind this injunction lies the fact that marriage is a picture of the relationship between Christ and his bride. And the Lord's commitment to his own people is exclusive and loyal. The prophet says, "as the bridegroom rejoices over the bride, so shall your God rejoice over you" (Isaiah 62:5). The Psalmist rejoices that "the LORD . . . does not forsake his saints; they are preserved forever" (Psalm 37:28). And the Lord passes on the same message to us, in Hebrews 13:5 for example, "I will never leave you nor forsake you." Samuel explained this commitment on God's part in these wonderful words: "the LORD will not forsake his people . . . because it has pleased the LORD to make you his people" (1 Samuel 12:22). How thankful we should be for the Lord's loyal love, and for the pleasure which he takes in us.

But now we move on to the third part of this section, 4:13–15. Here the topic is:

The Husband's Delight in his Wife

These verses explain why a wife is so lovable. She is like a lavish garden. In verses 13 and 14 we have a list of fruits and spices. They are the most expensive products of that day. In verse 12 the well was sealed. Now in verse 15 it is open—opened for the husband.

What this means is that when the wife is exclusively available for her husband and he for her, then you have a luscious experience of delight. Solomon's wife is the very epicentre of his happiness. God has built incalculable pleasure into marriage.

So we are challenged to consider where our values and priorities are. There is nothing more precious, nothing more calculated to promote happiness than love. So we must treat our spouse well. People are always very careful with their most treasured possessions. A spouse is infinitely precious. We must handle with care.

In so doing, of course, we reflect the tender delight which God finds in his beloved people. Just as 1 Peter 2:7 can say of Christ, "to you who believe, he is precious," so the Lord says of us, his people, "You shall no longer be termed Forsaken, nor shall your land any more be termed Desolate; but you shall be called Hephzibah [which means "my delight is in her"], and your land Beulah [which means "to be married"]; for the LORD delights in you, and your land shall be married" (Isaiah 62:4).

11

Love's Satisfaction Fulfilled

(Song of Solomon 4:16—5:1)

The theme of this pair of verses is the fulfilment of satisfaction which is found in married love. In the completion of love's passion in marriage there is deep satisfaction. You sense that as you read these two verses. They begin with a conversation between the wife and her husband. Verse 16 contains her words and he responds in the first part of verse 1.

First, she expresses the desire to be united in the intimacy of love. She invites her husband to let her garden become his garden, as she extols her own delicious attractiveness. He then describes that desire fulfilled, and expresses his satisfaction in having loved, and in continuing to love, his wife.

The last three lines of 5:1 are the second of the four places in the Song where I think someone other than the husband and wife are speaking. Who is speaking is not indicated because it is not important. What matters is who these words are spoken to, namely the lovers. They are being urged to eat up, and drink in, the joyful pleasure of love to the full. The words underline the wonderful satisfaction which is found in married love. The speakers are saying, Lose yourself in love for your spouse.

Deep satisfaction in marriage is God's design and intention. It is therefore to be enjoyed to the full. In the course of a marriage this satisfaction should be growing by the day. Let us seek to give and receive satisfaction in our love for our spouse. Here is something to be celebrated. Here is a reason to be thankful to the Creator.

And so we look up to heaven once more. The Scriptures portray a mutual satisfaction between God and his people. The Savior, we read, "shall see the labor of his soul, and be satisfied"; the rest of the verse tells us what that labor is: "my righteous Servant shall justify many, for he shall bear their iniquities" (Isaiah 53:11). And as Jesus looks out upon his justified people, he is satisfied, and it was "in his love and in his pity" that "he redeemed them" (Isaiah 63:9).

And just as the Savior finds satisfaction in his people, so we remember that there is no greater satisfaction to be found in all the world than that which we find in knowing that we are loved by God and in loving him in response. There are two Psalms which link our satisfaction with the Lord's love for us. Psalm 36:7 reads, "how precious is your lovingkindness, O God," and the next verse says that the children of men "are abundantly satisfied with the fullness of your house." And then Psalm 63:3 affirms, "your lovingkindness is better than life," and verse 5 draws out the implication: "My soul shall be satisfied as with marrow and fatness." And Psalm 17:15 looks forward to that future day when love's satisfaction will be consummated as we see Jesus face-to-face: "As for me, I will see your face in righteousness; I shall be satisfied when I awake in your likeness." Let us celebrate that love which we shall enjoy for all eternity.

12

Beware of Selfishness

(Song of Solomon 5:2—6:9)

Joyce Huggett wrote a number of books, including one entitled *Two into One: Growing in Christian Marriage.* In the preface she says this: "We are not offering a blue-print for a happy marriage. That would be foolish, for each marriage is as unique as the couple who unite to become 'one flesh.' Neither do we offer a guarantee of unmitigated joy. Few couples succeed in every aspect of their relationship."[1]

We have described the Song of Solomon as an idealized picture of marriage. Solomon in later years is looking back rather wistfully, realizing what his marriage might have been—if only. If only he had been faithful to one wife and not taken so many wives and concubines. The idealized picture holds before us a target to aim at in our marriages.

But to say that the Song presents an idealized picture of marriage is not to say that it is unrealistic or that reality is just ignored. As Joyce Huggett indicates, even in the best and happiest of marriages there are times of strain, tension, conflict, selfishness. And the Song of Solomon recognizes that. It does not give such an elevated portrait of married love that would leave us thinking either

1. Huggett, *Two into One*, 6.

83

that you can have a completely problem-free relationship, or that the goal is so unattainable that there is no point in even trying to aim for it. It may have been God's original ideal for relationships to be free from any tension, but the coming of sin into human life changed everything. Now, living as we do in a fallen world, if there is such a thing as an ideal marriage, it must be one that includes an exemplary approach to dealing with the problems in relationships.

In this section of the Song we are called to face up with realism to the fact that there are sometimes problems in marriages. Inevitably, in a world still marred by sin, stresses and strains will sometimes come into any marriage relationship.

In this passage we glimpse a marital difficulty, and then observe how it is dealt with. This means that we can divide the passage into two parts. First we see:

THE WOUNDING IMPACT OF
SELFISHNESS IN MARRIAGE (5: 2–9).

Throughout these verses we are hearing the voice of the wife. The second part of verse 2 actually contains her husband's words, but she is quoting him. In the final verse the daughters of Jerusalem, whom the wife addresses in verse 8, ask her a question, but probably the wife is really having a conversation with herself. She is imagining herself addressing the daughters of Jerusalem, and their reply continues the conversation taking place in her own mind.

In verse 2 Shulamite is in a drowsy state. Perhaps she has had a gruelling day. Her husband, by contrast, is wide awake, and eager to get his wife's attention. But in verse 3 she is quite reluctant. All she really wants to do is go to bed. She has already had a bath, and is not really in the mood for any sort of activity. But in verse 4 her husband gets very demanding, in spite of her reluctance. As a result, she slowly stirs herself, and in verse 5 we find her starting to respond to her husband, unlocking the door of her own longing for him. We see there something of the generosity of this wife, in responding to her husband, even though initially she had not felt up to it.

But in verse 6 it is all over. Her beloved has proved impatient, and no sooner has she started to respond than she finds that he has given up, turned his back, and gone. She is now searching for his love, but he is the one who has become unresponsive. She calls out to him, but gets no answer. And she is left feeling very much alone. And verse 7 amounts to the statement that she feels wounded by his demanding selfishness.

Surely this episode is included in the Song of Solomon as a rebuke to any man who sees his wife as existing merely for his own benefit, and who does not truly care for her needs. That is a danger in any marriage. We men can be very selfish. It is so easy just to take your wife for granted, to make unreasonable demands of her, to end up just using her for your own ends, instead of treating her as the equal which she ought to be. Men can wound their wives in spirit, and hardly notice. So Solomon is saying to husbands, beware, be careful.

So in verses 8 and 9 that imaginary conversation takes place between the wife and "the daughters of Jerusalem," representing the response that she makes to her own question within her own inner thoughts. She is torn in two. She is having a conversation with herself, and the gist of it is this: right now I can't find my beloved, he's unavailable; yet my desire for him has not been destroyed. And that raises the question, why? Why is he so precious, especially if he treats me like that? It is a bewildered question in the mind of a wife who feels wounded and alone.

And this leads us into the second part of the passage, which is all about:

THE RESOLUTION OF THE DIFFICULTY (5:10—6:9).

The resolution takes place in two stages, and, as with everything in the Song of Solomon, both parts of the resolution are conveyed in poetry and in picture, rather than by blunt statements. First we glimpse:

The Wife's Forgiveness (5:10—6:3).

The wife continues to speak in these verses. She begins by thinking about her husband. He has let her down right now, but she recalls that he is not always like that. In her generosity she turns over in her mind his good qualities.

In verse 10 Shulamite recognizes that her husband is second to none, "chief among ten thousand." Radiant whiteness and ruddiness represent respectively tenderness and strength. Just now the husband asserted his strength, but the tenderness was missing. But the wife remembers that it is not always so. And her very recollection of his tenderness towards her in the past is an act of forgiveness. That she can even recall it just then is evidence of her forgiving spirit.

From verse 11 through to the second line of verse 16, she pictures him. She looks at him in her mind's eye. The description which she gives represents the quality that she sees in him, and which she admires. According to verse 11 he has the value of gold and the darkness of manliness. In verse 12 she sees an attractive personality smiling at her through his eyes. In the first part of verse 13 she compares his cheeks to banks of flowers with their attractive scent. She might there be referring to his beard, which it was normal for a man to grow in those days. It was a mark of honor. The wife is saying, my husband is an honorable man. Then in the second half of the verse she recalls their pleasant times together, when his lips kissed her, and it was such a delectable sensation. Verse 14 mentions four valuable things. The wife sees her husband as a treasure. Verse 15 represents the man's dignity, and in verse 16 she remembers the many sweet things that he has said to her. Yes indeed, she sums up, "he is altogether lovely."

And she is saying all that when she has just been mistreated and left feeling wounded! Does that not represent forgiveness?

From the second half of verse 16 to the end of verse 3 we have another of those conversations between the wife and the "daughters of Jerusalem." Again, this is probably a conversation going on within her own mind.

It begins with a beautiful statement. Her beloved is her friend. Her commitment to go on cherishing friendship is an expression of the woman's forgiving nature.

Chapter 6 begins with a question: where has her husband gone? He is paying her no attention at that moment. But hear what the wife is able to say in verses 2–3. It amounts to this: I don't need to send out a search party; he's not really far away; I know that deep down he still loves me and enjoys me, and we belong together. She refers to his garden. We have seen that picture before: it symbolizes the wife herself. He is there in the garden, enjoying his wife. "I am my beloved's, and my beloved is mine."

So, there is the forgiveness of the wife. After being mistreated, she says, we are still one in the friendship of love.

Those of us who are husbands ought to reflect on the number of times that our wives have forgiven us over the years. We are probably totally unaware of many of the occasions. And yet, for all your selfishness, your wife is still there beside you. That is her forgiving nature.

This passage has the effect of reminding us what sort of husband every wife wants. She wants to see that combination of tenderness and strength. And there is a challenge to those of us who are husbands: have we found that balance? It is so easy for a husband to be strong in the demands he makes of his wife. But we need to be tender as well, not overbearing. The wife wants a leader in the home, but not a dictator. She wants a tender lover, though not a wimp.

What a tragedy it is in marriage if exploiting one another becomes an alternative to real, deep friendship. That sort of marriage is a travesty of what God intends. God said, "It is not good that man should be alone" (Genesis 2:18). As human beings we are made for a togetherness which embraces the whole of life, a togetherness in which husband and wife together share in enjoyment of all the everyday activities in which they take part side-by-side as friends. Solomon's wife is expressing the desire of every married woman. She wants a marriage that spells friendship in all the duties and pleasures of every day. But this is something that needs working at. A marriage which lacks friendship is a wounding experience.

We men need to recognize how amazing our wives are. How tolerant they are, how patient with us! What a lot they have to put up with! How selfish we can be! Yet they remain faithful, loyal, loving, forgiving. We must never forget to thank God for such a precious one. And never forget to thank her for putting up with you!

But now Solomon speaks, and we hear:

The Husband's Repentance (6:4–9).

His repentance is prompted by his wife's forgiveness. We imagine that he has just heard his wife's song of admiration and her protestation of loyalty to him. Her forgiving reaction to his selfishness causes his heart to melt in repentance, so that he praises her to the skies.

The reason why I think it is correct to take the whole of 5:2—6:9 as a single section is that 6:9 echoes 5:2. The words "my dove, my perfect one," are repeated. This is one of those ways in which the writer puts a sort of pair of brackets around the passage, as if to say, this is all one theme, all one section.

However, the repeated words are now heard in a new tone of voice. Back in 5:2 they were set in the context of selfish demand, as the husband said, "Open for me, . . . my dove, my perfect one." Now his heart is broken in repentance, and he speaks the same form of address with real admiration.

In verse 4 the husband's speech begins with reference to the beauty of his wife, not just physical beauty, but inner beauty. Tirzah is the name of a place in north Palestine, but it comes from a word meaning "to please." The husband finds the inner beauty of his wife's character so pleasing, especially her willingness to forgive.

At the start of verse 5 the husband thinks over his own selfishness. He just cannot bear at that moment the look of love that is coming out of her eyes. It has humbled him. It has overcome him. He has to ask her to look away.

Then, in the second half of that verse through to verse 7 he repeats some of his earlier words of admiration. We recognize the words from 4:1–3. The husband now feels the forgiveness that his wife has offered. He senses that he is forgiven, and that liberates him to express again his praise of her. He sums it up in verses 8 and 9 by saying that she is simply unique. There is no one like her. He just cannot imagine anyone else being so magnanimous, so generous, so forgiving.

What we have in verses 4–9 is an illustration of how the wife's generosity has brought her husband low in repentance, but also lifted him up again. And now he is free once more to admire his wife without embarrassment.

And so we remember that the love of husband and wife portrayed here points us upwards once again to the highest love of all—that love of God in Christ for his church. An Old Testament illustration is never an exact reflection of the standard which we find in Christ. We speak of David as a type of Christ, but that doesn't mean that Jesus committed adultery as David did. An illustration is a pointer, and sometimes, as in this instance, it points by way of contrast. There is a love which is never selfish, a love which is always giving and forgiving, a love which never merely exploits. We should be very grateful that we have a Savior who was so selfless that in love he gave up his life for his people. That is the standard against which we should measure our love for one another. And like the wife in the Song, we, the bride of Christ, should be overflowing in admiration for him.

13

Awesome Privilege

(Song of Solomon 6:10—7:5)

In the previous passage, we suggested that the husband was guilty of taking his wife for granted, treating her selfishly, making unreasonable demands of her. This had a wounding impact on his wife. The damaged situation was resolved by her forgiveness and his repentance. Now we find that he has learned his lesson. In this passage he celebrates the awesome privilege of married love.

Throughout this section, for the most part the husband is speaking. He says everything except the last two lines of verse 13, which are the words of the wife. In that verse the two of them have a brief conversation, which makes up verse 13 as a whole.

The section begins with Solomon pondering. In verse 10 he asks, "who is she?" He means, what sort of woman is this, so selfless that she can find such grace to forgive? She is indeed so awe-inspiring.

Back in chapter 5 verse 2, Solomon addressed his wife in a demanding and self-centred tone, "open for me." But now, in verse 11, he is no longer making a demand for her time. Rather, he is engaged in an exploration. He is trying to assess whether his wife is ready and willing to give him of her time and energy. He is investigating;

he is trying to see what is realistic, what is fair. The garden here, as usual in the Song of Solomon, is a symbol of the wife. The buds and the blooms represent her willingness to be available to spend time with her husband. He is not demanding her attention, but is pausing to find out whether she feels up to spending some time in the aloneness of love.

In verse 12, he is so excited to discover that she is eager to spend intimate time with him. In fact, her response to his approach was so rapid and instantaneous that Solomon is overwhelmed by the sense of privilege at being able to be so close to another person, to have such access into another person's life. He feels as if he is a nobleman riding in a luxurious chariot.

To ride in a chariot in those days was certainly a sign of great honor and prestige. When Joseph was made second in command in Egypt after Pharaoh, we read that Pharaoh had Joseph "ride in the second chariot which he had; and they cried out before him, 'Bow the knee!'" (Genesis 41:43). To be in the chariot was a symbol of the unexpected honor that had come to Joseph there in Egypt. By using this picture, Solomon is saying that for a husband, to be in this position where your wife allows you to be so intimately close to her is an honor, a privilege which the husband has no right to take for granted.

Here again we hear a challenge to those of us who are husbands. We must never forget what a privilege it is to be admitted into the place of seclusion with our wife. We must never take it for granted. We all prize our personal space. We dislike it if someone intrudes on that space. Marriage is a real privilege, because it involves the husband's intrusion on his wife's personal space. The fact that she is willing is a great honor.

I remember a friend once telling me that what she had found most difficult to cope with when she first got married was the loss of privacy. There was another person there all the time, and that was hard to get used to. A husband needs to be sensitive to his wife's feelings in this respect. We must count it a great privilege to live under the same roof, to share the same space, as another person. We must be ready to give space and private time when necessary, though without ever using that as an excuse for neglect, of course. It certainly is a privilege for the husband to enjoy married love.

And now the rest of this section indicates that this sense of privilege in married love is there for the wife as well. Verse 13 is in the plural: this is clear from the word "we" in the first half of the verse, but the word "you" in the second part is also plural (in the question, "what would you see in the Shulamite?"). Nonetheless, I think that it is still only the husband and wife having a conversation. He speaks, then she replies, and they are talking excitedly about the love they share. We might call it a plural of emotion or elation.

In this verse the husband is full of admiration for his wife. He wants to look upon her again and again, and again and again—so four times he repeats the call, "return." Shulamite is so enticing, so appealing to him. But look at her reaction: what can you see in me? Shulamite asks him.

Shulamite knows that there are certain things in life which are real spectacles. As far as she is concerned, she would happily be a spectator at a dance. "The two camps" was the name given by Jacob to the place where the angels met him as he was on his way to meet up with Esau. We read about it in Genesis 32:2. The New King James Version uses the Hebrew name, Mahanaim, there, but the footnote explains it as meaning literally "Double Camp." Here in the Song of Solomon it is translated slightly differently, but it is clear enough that two camps and a double camp amount to pretty much the same thing. But why does Shulamite speak of "the dance of the two camps"? Very probably, in the course of history since Jacob's time, a particular dance routine had been invented there, and had become known as "the dance of Mahanaim," "the dance of the two camps." To watch a performance of that dance was evidently quite a spectacle. Shulamite loves it, and maybe her husband is a keen fan too. But what she cannot understand just now is why her husband should find the same pleasure in looking at her. This is the modesty of the woman. She is genuinely surprised that she should be such an object of admiration.

Many a wife has that same reserve about herself. She may have no difficulty in understanding her husband's desire to cheer from the terraces on a Saturday afternoon, but the fact that he then comes home and wants to cheer for her as well makes her feel like asking, but what on earth do you see in me?

Immediately her husband answers. The first five verses of chapter 7 are her husband saying, Let me tell you what I see in you, so that you can understand why I want to look upon you again and again, and again and again.

In these verses he is looking at her body, and highlighting her physical attractiveness. He starts at her feet in verse 1 and moves his eyes upwards to her head in verse 5. In between he looks admiringly at her thighs (also in verse 1), her navel and her waists in verse 2, her breasts (verse 3), her neck, her eyes, and her nose in verse 4, and then also the hair on her head in verse 5. And it is all so beautiful, so alluring to him. It is like scrutinizing rich jewels (verse 1), like sampling a goblet of the best wine (verse 2). It is all so well proportioned, he says, again in verse 2: "your waist is a heap of wheat" (men in those days didn't much admire girls who were slim sylphs). In verse 4 we have some further vivid descriptions. The wife is elegant, like a castle built of ivory. She is a source of tranquillity: Heshbon is a place name, and Bath Rabbim was one of its gates; it was a place famous for pools of water which were exceptionally still. What is more, Shulamite is stately: the thing about the tower of Lebanon was its straightness. This flattering yet sincere adulation continues into verse 5. Shulamite's beauty is lush: Mount Carmel was known for the lavishness of its vegetation. She bears the marks of royalty. It all adds up to this: what a wonder you are! No wonder that I so admire you and want to look upon you, to gaze and gaze at you, so much.

The husband is aiming to lift his wife above those feelings of littleness which she expressed in her question. He says, don't be so down on yourself, don't belittle yourself; you're wonderful. He wants to lift her up above those self-effacing instincts, to reassure her of how acceptable and how wonderful her personality is. He wants to convince her that it is a privilege for him as a husband to be with her, and so she begins to feel the privilege of married love as well.

Once again we husbands need to consider the challenge of this passage. Is it not true that many women sometimes have feelings of personal inadequacy, insecurity, lack of confidence? And the husband's job is to boost his wife's sense of worth in being herself, to elevate her, to lift her up to a sense of her womanly glory. The key to that, as Solomon knew, is to speak words of praise and adoration and admiration, backed up by actions of tender, imaginative romance.

We must always remember this, that in admiring his wife, a husband is admiring the skilful handiwork of God. In the last line of verse 1 the husband describes his wife as "the work of the hands of a skillful workman." If a husband fails to admire his wife, he is really insulting the Creator, the skillful workman who made her. So how careful we need to be to make sure that we are admiring husbands.

But now it is time to remind ourselves that the human love portrayed in this Song is intended to point us upwards to that highest love of all.

Most of what this passage signals is how astonishing a thing it is that we should be loved so much by our Lord. Like the wife in the Song, we may frequently wonder how on earth the holy Lord could love us so much, or even at all. We continue to be aware of our shortcomings, our failures. Our sins still get the better of us so often. How can there be any glory for God in having the likes of us as his people? Surely we are a burden that he has to bear, not a privilege that he longs to enjoy. And yet we must not fall into the trap of a false humility which denies the grace of God towards us.

The fact is that, just as Solomon compared Shulamite to rich jewels, so the Lord says that we are his jewels. Listen to these words from Malachi 3:16–17:

> Then those who feared the LORD spoke to one another,
> And the LORD listened and heard them;
> So a book of remembrance was written before him
> For those who fear the LORD
> And who meditate on his name.
> "They shall be Mine," says the LORD of hosts,
> "On the day that I make them my jewels."

It is indeed a tremendous privilege for us all to be loved by God, and yet as he says to us, "I have loved you with an everlasting love; therefore with lovingkindness I have drawn you" (Jeremiah 31:3). And these are the words of that ultimate in skillful workmen, the Creator of the whole world. He so loved the world which he had formed and shaped, he so loved us, the creatures whom he had made in his own image, that he gave his only Son to be the Savior of the world, to rescue his image from the damage done by sin, and to restore us to his heart and his warm embrace, to remould us with his skilful hands into the likeness of the Son of his love.

Is our breath taken away by the privilege of having that love showered upon us? Or have we lost something of the sense of wonder?

But this passage began with Solomon, having learned his lesson, waiting patiently for his wife's willing response to his overtures of love. Now, of course, our heavenly lover never needs to learn a lesson and correct a hasty intrusion. But in learning that lesson, Solomon's love was re-shaped according to the likeness of the love of the Lord. In his love for us God is exceedingly patient. He longs for fellowship with us every single day, but he does not force himself upon us. He waits patiently for our readiness to respond to him. The Lord Jesus Christ wants us to love him willingly, not reluctantly. We have the responsibility to cultivate nearness of fellowship to him. It ought to be our constant prayer that the Holy Spirit will awaken genuine longing for God in our hearts, so that we respond to him with eager desire. In the case of Shulamite—and any other human wife for that matter—there may well be times when hesitancy about conforming to her husband's desires for intimate seclusion is a valid response. But what a sad thing it would be if we ever feel that the felt presence of the Lord as a daily reality is an unrealistic dream, or if we are too preoccupied with other things to bother about intimacy with the Lord, and therefore do nothing to seek to cultivate the sense of walking with the Lord in all the intricate details of daily life every day. Let us all take care that we do not become content with keeping the Lord at a distance.

14

A Catalog of Delights

(Song of Solomon 7:6)

The next verse (7:6) stands alone. It speaks of the abundant joys of married love. Ariel and Chana Bloch describe it as "an enthusiastic paean."[1]

Once again we have here the husband's words. He is not now speaking to his wife, but to love itself. The word translated "love" here is not the same word which the husband constantly uses when he addresses his wife as "my love," as, for example, in 6:4. This word means love itself, and Solomon is highlighting the joys of love by addressing love.

Delitzsch comments that "there is nothing more admirable than love," which he proceeds to define in the present context as "the uniting or mingling together of two lives, the one of which gives itself to the other, and so finds the complement of itself." Love, he continues, is both "self-devotion," and "self-enrichment."[2]

It is noteworthy how the verse speaks of "the delights" of love—in the plural. Solomon is aware that the joys found in love are manifold and incomparable. Nothing else in all the world is equivalent.

1. Bloch and Bloch, *Song*, 204.
2. Delitzsch, *Song*, 129.

The Hebrew word behind "with" in the second line of this verse is open to several possible translations, and there is no doubt truth in all the options.

Ariel and Chana Bloch suggest the word "among:"[3] "How fair and how pleasant you are, O love, among the delights." In other words, there are many delights in life—good food, good wine, sport, the countryside. But amongst them all, the fairest and most pleasant is to be in love with your spouse.

The Authorized Version translates using the word "for:" "How fair and how pleasant you are, O love, for delights!" This rendering suggests that everybody is looking for delights out of life. We do not want a joyless existence. So where are we to turn in this quest for delights? How are we to find what will make us truly happy? The answer for the married person is to be in love with your spouse. That is where you will find delights abundant!

The Living Bible also opts for the word "for," and translates rather vividly: "Oh, how delightful you are, how pleasant, O love, for utter delight!"

Several other versions, as well as the New King James, use the word "with." This emphasizes the truth that to be in love with your spouse is to discover that love does not come on its own. It brings with it a whole packet of joys.

Whichever translation you go for, this verse really sums up the whole celebratory emphasis which runs right through the Song of Solomon. This verse is an ode in praise of love itself. The delights of love are incomparable and innumerable.

And obviously, such a statement drives us upwards yet again. We remember that for delights surpassing everything, even the joys of human love, it is the love of God which is the most beautiful and the most pleasant of all. To know and to feel that the Son of God died for your sins should make you burst with appreciative joy. Never lose the sense of the delight in that love.

On one occasion Jesus used a word related to the one they chose here when they translated the Old Testament into Greek. In Luke 7:24–25 he contrasts John the Baptist as "a reed shaken by the

3. Bloch and Bloch, *Song*, 204.

wind" with those "those who are gorgeously apparelled and live in luxury"; they are "in kings' courts," he says. It is the word translated "luxury" that we are interested in. In this context Jesus is not commending luxury: John the Baptist, for all his ruggedness, was far greater than those who live in the lap of luxury. But here in the Song of Solomon, it is recognized that when the luxuries which we are talking about are the luxurious experiences of married love, then that is a delightful reality, and we have no need to feel embarrassed about it. In the same way, to enjoy and appreciate the love of God in Christ is emphatically to feel that you have all the luxuries in life that you could ever desire. With Jesus at your side, life is a whole catalog of delights.

15

Love Freely Given

(Song of Solomon 7:7–12)

I suppose that it is a golden rule that love cannot be taken, it can only be given. That is why it is such a privilege and such a joy. This section builds up to the climax of the very last line, where the wife says, "I will give you my love." This summarizes the theme of the whole passage, which is the gift of married love.

As far as the first line of verse 9 the husband is speaking. The rest of the passage is the wife's response to what her husband has said.

The passage begins with the husband thinking back to the days before they were married. Ariel and Chana Bloch point out that the Hebrew verbs here are in a form denoting a past tense.[1] So the beginning of verse 7 would be better rendered, "This stature of yours was like a palm tree." The husband is recalling to himself the time when he was first getting to know the girl who was to become his wife. At that time she was inaccessible. That is the significance of the picture of the palm tree.

Have you ever seen a palm tree on your travels? I have had the privilege of seeing coconut palms both in the Seychelles and

1. Bloch and Bloch, *Song*, 205.

in the Philippines. They are graceful and beautiful, and so was this girl, though Solomon probably has in mind the date, rather than the coconut, palm. A date palm produces sweet fruits. So there was a sweetness of nature about this girl that the husband-to-be was beginning to admire. But palm trees are also very tall, and the leaves and fruit begin only a few inches from the top. The only way to pick the fruit is to climb a ladder. And this beautiful young woman at that time was out of reach. The time for love's intimacy has not yet arrived.

There is just another hint of this warning that surfaces in the Song from time-to-time. There is a right situation, a proper place, for physical love. Before that time and place come it is out of bounds.

But in the first two lines of verse 8 we have the young man resolving that he is going to court this woman. She may be out of reach just yet, but somehow he will win her heart. And in the third line of the verse we move from how it used to be then to how it is now. Now everything is different. Now she is no longer inaccessible like that huge palm tree with its clusters of dates way out of reach. She is now like a vine with its clusters of grapes close to hand. Now it is possible to cuddle up to her and enjoy her kisses, because now they are married. And as for her kisses, well, they are like the very best wine, as the first line of verse 9 says.

At this point the wife chips in. She takes up what he has just said about her kisses. She says, it's quite right that he should have my love and kisses. And why? Because they belong together. The word translated "desire" in verse 10 occurs in only two other places in the Bible. In Genesis 3:16 God said to the woman after sin had come into the world, "Your desire shall be for your husband, and he shall rule over you." In Genesis 4:7, God said to Cain when his offering had been rejected and he was beginning to feel anger towards Abel, "If you do not do well, sin lies at the door. And its desire is for you, but you should rule over it." In both contexts the word means the desire for mastery, for conquest, for control.

When God spoke to the woman in Genesis 3, he was saying, there will be this tendency in you to desire to control your husband, but I am not going to allow it; I have appointed the man to be the ruler. In the Song of Solomon we see how, in the beauty of married love, the curse that was placed on the fallen world is to some extent overcome and reversed. Here the wife is not saying, I desire my husband, I desire to rule and conquer him. She is saying, his desire is towards me. But, of course, in this context, it is not the desire of power and control, but the desire of love. That is the proper way for a husband to rule in his marriage—in love. And married love, when lived according to God's pattern, reverses the curse that God placed on the world at the beginning. Here the wife happily submits to her husband's desire. She expresses that submission in the invitation of verse 11, where, in picture language, she invites him to the field of love.

In verse 12 she says that there is no longer any need to wait. We are married, we can enjoy one another intimately whenever we want to. In the second, to fourth lines of the verse the wife echoes the words which her husband had spoken in chapter 6 verse 11. He was enquiring, are you in the mood, are you ready for us to be together in love's seclusion? Now she repeats the question as her way of saying, yes, indeed, I am. So she gives him her love.

We have spoken, then, of the gift of love. And I think the tragedy of brokenness in relationships, which happens so sadly frequently, occurs when one of the couple thinks that love is a right which may be taken. But it is not. None of us should think that we have the right to another person's love in such intimacy. None of us should imagine that we deserve the love of another person. Love is a privilege which has to be given, and we need to remember that in our marriages. And when we receive that gift, then, like the couple in the Song, we need to be truly grateful and appreciative. So the Song of Solomon says to us, celebrate. Thank God for married love, and do not forget to thank your spouse as well.

And once again God's own love is the model. There is nothing that we can do to secure that love. We do not have any right to be loved by God. That is why we speak of his grace. It means that he freely gives his love to the undeserving. All that we can do is to receive the love that is offered, and we receive it through faith in Jesus Christ.

16

Inseparable Togetherness

(Song of Solomon 7:13—8:6a)

I don't know whether you have noticed, but there is not a single reference to God anywhere in the Song of Solomon. God is never mentioned. But in an article on the Song, John Richardson writes: "When God is located nowhere specifically, it may not be because he is *completely absent*, but rather because he is *everywhere present*."[1] We know, of course, that God is everywhere present in our lives, in the entire universe. We live our whole life before God. That does not exclude any part of our lives, not even the most private, intimate part, the married life, which the Song has been discussing. God observes that aspect of our life, and he means us to enjoy it and to fulfil our responsibilities in connection with it.

When Adam and Eve sinned in the Garden of Eden they felt shame for the first time. Even though they had been naked in each other's presence they had not felt shame before. But sinned damaged human emotion, and brought shame where previously there had been none. In Christ all our shame has gone because our sin is forgiven. We are free again to enjoy our humanity as God intends it to be. And what comes through very strongly in the Song

---

1. Richardson, "Preaching from the *Song*," 138 (italics original).

of Solomon is that one thing which God intends in terms of our enjoyment of our humanity is that sexual relations are reserved for marriage.

And that is where this passage begins. It divides into two sections, and the theme of the first part is:

INTENSE LONGING (7:13—8:4).

This is another of the flashback passages. The woman speaks, but we are looking back to the days before the wedding. At that time she and Solomon are the ancient equivalent of an engaged couple. She is looking forward to the marriage which has been arranged, and which will be coming up before very long.

She starts by referring to mandrakes. You have probably not got any of those in your garden. In fact, maybe we did not even realize that a mandrake was the name of a plant. But it was, and it was nicknamed the "love plant." It was believed in ancient times that it had some association with love. Some people even believed that it would enhance your love life if you ate it. But, more important in this context, a mandrake had an appealing, exotic fragrance. And what Shulamite intends to say here is that marriage, with all its joys, which at this stage she is anticipating for the future, certainly has an appeal for her already. She is looking forward, with great excitement, to the day of her wedding.

She speaks, as it were, to her fiancé, of the gateway into her heart. She says "our gates," because she is on the point of sharing the whole of herself with her beloved. She is anticipating complete union. In that union there are choice fruits to enjoy. There are old fruits, because already in courtship and engagement they have been able to enjoy just so much of each other's company. But there will be new fruits as well once they are married—things which are not available until marriage comes. The old fruits include excited emotions, the longing to be together, spending time chatting, walking—whatever engaged couples do. The new fruit will be the permanent togetherness, the consummation of the relationship, once the marriage is sealed.

The woman is quite clear that with the coming of the new (the fulfilment of marriage) she does not want to lose the old. The best marriages are those where the emotions and activities of courtship continue alongside the deeper intimacy which is possible after the wedding. It is a great shame if the joys of courtship fall away once you get married. Throughout marriage we should always be enjoying the old aspects of the relationship, whilst remembering that there is always something new to discover and enjoy in the new intimacy of relationship between husband and wife. We need to work hard at making sure that things do not degenerate so that marriage becomes nothing but a chore, and all the old things that we enjoyed when we were courting have gone. That would be a tragic situation. The woman here, looking forward to her marriage wants to hold on to the old things as well as to enjoy the new. She speaks of having laid up these fruits for her beloved. She has stored them up, reserved them for him. Every married couple should make this same commitment to exclusiveness.

In verse 1 of chapter 8 this looking forward deepens into an even more intense longing. She says, in effect, Oh that you were like a brother to me. Four times in chapters 4 and 5 the man referred to "my sister, my spouse," where "sister" is equivalent to "wife." This is a way of speaking of the closeness of the marriage relationship. There is something special in a relationship between a brother and a sister. At least there should be, and usually there is. I know that some men do not get on with their sisters and vice versa, but generally speaking, I think, there is a deep bond between a brother and a sister which survives long beyond the days of childhood, and maybe even becomes stronger as adulthood progresses. And in marriage there is a closeness which cannot be known in human relationships otherwise, except in the brother-sister relationship. And even in those cases where that deep subjective brother-sister bond is missing, which we have to acknowledge does sadly happen sometimes, the objective reality is still that brother and sister are family. And when you get married, you certainly become family with someone new. So here, Shulamite means, Oh that you were already my husband. I can hardly wait. I want a relationship which is as close as that of a brother and sister who were fed with the same mother's milk; I want us, as soon as possible, to be family.

She goes on to explain her reason: if the two of them should be together outside, in a public place, they could have a kiss without anyone despising them. For a courting couple, even an engaged couple, there are limits to what is appropriate behavior in public. To kiss in the street, certainly in those days, if you were only engaged, was regarded as not quite proper. Even today people despise an excessive display of emotion on the part of courting couples. It is an embarrassment.

But when you are married it is different. You are more restrained anyway, because you are more mature. But even so there is no embarrassment about hugs and kisses even in public places. There is no fear or shame. "I would not be despised," Shulamite says. So she longs for that day when there will be this intimacy which she need not have any shame about, because she will be with her husband. The marriage will have taken place.

On that day, according to verses 2 and 3, it will be perfectly legitimate for her to take her man home and put into practice what her mother has taught her. She is talking here about enjoying the spiced wine and the fruit juice of married love.

Verse 3 repeats words first heard in chapter 2 verse 6. But the context is different now. There Shulamite was speaking as a woman already married, and describing the pleasure which she derived from her husband's embrace. Here she is still looking forward to that loving embrace. That is how it would be if only we were married, is her thought. We are not yet, but one day soon we will be. And Shulamite longs intensely for that day.

Verse 2 speaks of "the house of my mother." We have come across that phrase before, in chapter 3 verse 4, where it referred to the place where the wedding arrangements were finalized. Here, though, it is the mother's role as teacher which is highlighted. Part of the finalizing of the marriage arrangements involved the mother's teaching about the life of a wife, about the desire, the submission, and all that is involved in marriage for a woman. Shulamite is looking forward to the day when that teaching can be put into practice.

There is something worth noting there. Solomon is assuming that the responsibility for sex education is parental. As always, God's wisdom is beyond question. Our society has given the responsibility for sex education by and large to others than parents. And perhaps we are reaping the consequences of that these days, especially now that our society seems to have descended into what Deuteronomy 28:28 calls "madness and blindness and confusion of heart" as far as gender and all the associated issues are concerned.

Throughout Scripture the responsibility for the education of children belongs to parents. That is not necessarily an argument against schools, though there is much to respect in the Home Education movement. But we do need to remember that the authority of a school is the delegated authority of parents. A school has no independent authority beyond that. A school is a request which parents make for help in a task which they cannot perform entirely on their own. You could call it a parents' co-operative. Strictly speaking, morally speaking, biblically speaking, the state has no valid jurisdiction in this realm.

But even if we allow that there is a role for schools as delegated by parents, there are still some things which are best left to be dealt with at home, and one of them is sex education. Maybe there would be far fewer moral problems in society if it were the mothers who instructed, rather than somebody else.

So here is the engaged young woman musing in anticipation of how it will be once they are married, and how it would be now if they were already married, and thinking, with this intense longing, O that it were so. But in verse 4 she recognizes that it is not like that yet. Here is a third repetition of this warning against premature lovemaking. Premature lovemaking does not please: it brings displeasure with it. Here, perhaps, she is speaking to herself as one of the daughters of Jerusalem. She is saying to herself, as an engaged woman, Be careful; don't let yourself be carried away to your own ruin; the day for the fulfilment of married love is not yet, because you're still only engaged.

And so the time has come to raise our vision upwards to the love between Jesus and his church. Shulamite, who is speaking here, is the counterpart of the church, Christ's bride-to-be. I trust that we do know something of that intensity of longing reflected in this passage for the day when we shall see our Savior and finally be united to him inseparably forever, when everything will be fully shared with him. I hope we find the thought that we shall be with him for all eternity as appealing as Shulamite finds the prospect of marriage. We need to make sure that we are enjoying walking with the Lord in spirit now (enjoying the old fruits), and that we are filled with desire for the day when we shall enter into a new dimension of love with him.

But let us remember, too, that throughout eternity we shall be enjoying ever more blessed experiences of mutual love for our Lord. We must not imagine that heaven will be static, like some kind of eternal motionlessness. I do not think that it will be like that at all. In eternity heaven will be growth and development, and every day experiencing yet a higher level of love, infinitely, forever. The final chapter of Sam Storms's book, *One Thing*, is entitled "Joy's Eternal Increase." He speaks of the blessedness of heaven as "progressive, incremental, and incessantly expansive." He says this:

> As the rain of revelation and insight and discovery continues to fall throughout the endless ages of eternity, so the water level of love and joy and happiness rises higher and higher, never to abate or to any degree diminish.[2]

Every day, for ever and ever, we shall plumb new depths of love which will entice us onwards into an endless infinity of spiritual experience. It is indescribable, but it certainly will not be boring!

Just as Shulamite anticipates a relationship as close as that between a brother and a sister, so we remember that the Son of God who became fully human is our older brother, that in him we are adopted as younger siblings into the family of God, and the one who has shown us the ultimate in brotherly love is the very one to whom we shall be united in heavenly marriage forever.

The reference to the mother's instruction is interesting, because in earlier days, and in some circles even now, Christians would speak of the "mother church." It is a term which depicts the church as a mother "in her functions of nourishing and protecting

2. Storms, *One Thing*, 170.

the believer."[3] An important role of the church is to instruct believers as to how we are to put our love for Jesus into practice now, and to teach us to anticipate that day of glory when we shall see him face-to-face. The manual for the church's teaching is, of course, the Bible, and just as, in an ideal world at any rate, parents would be able to ensure that schools are held to account and only teach what is right, so God's Word is our protection against being taken in by all the errors of our culture and our time, so that our intense longing for Jesus is sustained. Psalm 107:9 assures us that "he satisfies the longing soul." So we need to ensure that our souls are filled with longing for him.

So we have thought about the intense longing of engagement. But, of course, the happy day does come at last, and that brings us to the second theme of this section, which we entitle:

TOGETHER AT LAST (8:5–6A).

The first part of verse 5 gives us the briefest snippet of a wedding scene, as it echoes words from the longer wedding scene in 3:6. This is the third of those four places where I judge that someone other than Solomon and Shulamite is speaking. One of the wedding guests exclaims: "Who is this coming up from the wilderness, leaning upon her beloved?"

So now the two are united. Now the wedding has taken place. Shulamite is leaning upon Solomon without any embarrassment. No one despises her. They are husband and wife.

In the rest of verse 5 and the first two lines of verse 6 the wife speaks of what follows.

The wedding night is described in verse 5. The wife has awakened the husband's desire. Her very attractiveness, her beauty, has aroused his longing for intimate union with her. Back in 2:3 Shulamite spoke of her husband himself as the apple tree. Now she says that they are under the apple tree, and that this is the place where his desire is awakened. It is a delicate picture of married love, and she is celebrating the fact that to be united to him in married

3. Wikipedia, *Mother Church*, para. 1.

love is to be in the very same position that his own mother was, in such a union, the result of which was his coming into existence in the first place. The repeated "there," in the last two lines of verse 5, refers not to the identical place, but to an identical relationship.

But the vital thing about marriage is referred to in the opening lines of verse 6. The wife is saying, now that the wedding has taken place, we are inseparable. A seal stamped an item as belonging to a particular person. To describe herself in these terms, is a way in which the wife says, you belong to me, we belong together. There is total belonging, complete sharing, unrestricted access into each other's presence, because we belong as man and wife.

Before my wife and I got married, Paul Cook, the pastor who conducted our wedding, said to us, "Marriage is the total end of the single life." Once you are married everything changes. You are no longer one, but two. Life is shared in every aspect. And that is what Shulamite is saying here. The wedding vows have been made, and the two are bound together for life. That is true both in private ("a seal upon your heart"—where it is invisible), and in public ("a seal upon your arm"—which is visible). Both in the secret life of the husband and wife alone, and in their joint life lived out in the world, the single life is over. When this total belonging has taken place, then whether you are at home alone—just the two of you, or whether you are mixing in company, you belong together, and nothing can separate you. And there is no shame in that, no embarrassment about being together in public.

Maybe there is a note of warning here too. I once read a report on a study by some psychologists. They had concluded that an early sign of a marriage in difficulty is seen in facial expression. When one of the couple says something, the face of the other expresses disgust. Or one of the couple does something, and in the face of the other you can see disdain.

We are reminded here that in this relationship of total belonging to each other mutual respect is vital. We must never lose the ability to go on gazing starry eyed at our loved one, however old we get. There is no embarrassment whatsoever about being together, accepting one another, because we are sealed as belonging to each other. There must be no disdain or disgust at what our spouse does. This is what the Song of Solomon calls us to aim at.

And again, this Song points us upwards to the higher love, the highest love of all—God's inseparable commitment to us, his people. The thing about God's love is that he will never abandon his own. Even in days when his ancient people were recalcitrant and rebellious, "bent on backsliding," as Hosea 11:7 puts it, the Lord responds with this remarkable statement in verses 8–9:

> How can I give you up, Ephraim?
> *How* can I hand you over, Israel?
> How can I make you like Admah?
> *How* can I set you like Zeboiim?
> My heart churns within me;
> My sympathy is stirred.
> I will not execute the fierceness of my anger;
> I will not again destroy Ephraim.
> For I *am* God, and not man,
> The Holy One in your midst;
> And I will not come with terror.

Those are wonderful words which assure us too that whatever our past may have been, that however much we stumble along the way, the Lord's loving commitment is secure, and he will never again come against his people with anger. Jesus bore the full brunt of God's holy anger against our sin when he died on the cross. And realizing that this is true challenges us to be committed to him in response with lifelong commitment. That is what being a Christian in love with the Lord really means.

And when we feel the power of God's commitment to his people, evoking commitment from us to him, then we can come back down to earth, and seek to put the same thing into practice in our marriages. This sense of inseparability linked with the fulfilment of desire springs from the joy of married love.

In my view, the rest of the Song of Solomon, from the third line of verse 6 onwards, is the fourth and final place where we hear other voices. That means that these first two lines of verse 6 are the last words spoken by Solomon and Shulamite. We could say, then, that this is the point at which the Song of Solomon, at least as concerns the marriage of this particular couple, reaches its climax. And the climax is reached in this statement that we are inseparable now; we belong. That is the heart of what marriage is all about.

And it is also the heart of what salvation is all about—that we shall be for ever inseparable from the one to whom we now eternally belong—our Lord Jesus Christ.

17

Love—powerful, passionate, and priceless

(Song of Solomon 8:6b–7)

We mentioned in an earlier chapter that in the Hebrew Bible the Song of Solomon is included in the "Wisdom Literature." This category includes the books of Job, Psalms, Proverbs, and Ecclesiastes as well. Their main aim is to teach us about human life and human experience in the light of the basic truth that *God is*. They are talking about how we understand human life, given that God is the Creator and the ever-present Lord in his creation. The question which they set out to answer is, how can we make sense of our experience? After all, as Job tells us, there are times when it just does not make sense, or doesn't seem to. This provoked him to ask, "Where is the place of understanding?" (Job 28:12). What is life all about? What things really matter? How can we know God?

Well, one aspect of our human experience in the light of God's reality is the love of a man for a woman. But the Song of Solomon is a bit different from most of the Wisdom Literature, just because it is a song. It is true that there are many poetic sections in the other Wisdom Literature books too, and that the Psalms are songs, but only the Song of Solomon is written as one continuous cycle of poems. As we have been seeing, most of it is an illustration. It is describing a relationship, not giving us ground rules for relationships, except in so far as we can work them out from what is actually happening in the love between this man, Solomon, and this woman, his wife, Shulamite.

However, this verse and a half (8:6b–7) is an exception to that. Here it seems that a narrator speaks. Just for a moment we are not looking into this particular relationship between Solomon and Shulamite, as the rest of the book up to this point has done, but hearing a general statement about love, a more abstract summary of what the Song has all been about.

These verses speak of love in general. They are a reflection on the nature of love itself. All the rest of the book so far has illustrated and celebrated love. But here is a statement about love, and it presents us with the key to the whole book. All the rest of the book so far has illustrated the truth which is now made explicit in this statement. In hearing this declaration about love we are being invited to rejoice in the experience of love which is given to us by God. From this short passage we learn three things.

LOVE IS POWERFUL

"Love is as strong as death." Death is inescapable. It overpowers everybody in the end, from the lowest to the greatest. Cleverness will not protect you from death. Position will not preserve you from death. Money cannot insure you against death.

In the same way, love is a universal human reality. There is a driving power within us. God has made us to love. Once our heart is conquered, love overpowers us. However manly we may be, love is irresistible. It is just part of the way we are as human beings.

This of course points us to God. We are made in God's image, and when the Son of God came into the world to save lost and hopeless sinners, he was overpowered by love. That is what drove him to give himself on the cross.

That being so, we have no reason for shame when the urge to love our husband / our wife takes possession of us. It is simply a reflection of the Creator who made us.

Solomon points out that the power of love is expressed in jealousy. He describes jealousy as a raging fire, a vehement flame. Here is the possessiveness which is an essential part of true love. The sense of rage if love is betrayed is quite right and proper. God himself said in Exodus 20:3 and 5, "You shall have no other gods before me . . . for I, the LORD your God, am a jealous God." God will have his people for himself. He will be affronted when they go after other gods. And in just the same way, when a man and a woman have been united in love, there will be outrage if one or other breaks that bond. A love which does not have that jealousy about it is a very weak and wimpish sort of love, and hardly worthy of the name.

The apostle Paul spoke to the Corinthians about his jealousy for them. He says, "I have betrothed you to one husband" (2 Corinthians 11:2). The preaching of the gospel had resulted in their being married to Christ. So Paul says, I am jealous that you remain faithful.

Jealousy, we are told furthermore, is "cruel as the grave." That means that it is unyielding. In Proverbs 30:16 the grave is listed as one of four things that never say, "It is enough." The other three are the barren womb, the earth that is not satisfied with water, and the fire. A fire will keep burning as long as there are things to burn. The earth will never be finished with receiving the waters of the rain that fall upon it. A childless couple crave a child. And the grave is never satisfied: not until every human being who ever lived has died will the grave close its deadly mouth.

And jealousy is as relentless as the grave. Where husband and wife are united in this powerful love, they have so taken possession of each other that they are never satisfied. They are always eager for more. And if one of the couple betrays their love, the other will be rightly angry to the point that he or she would prefer it if the spouse were dead. And that is just what God intended.

So we are invited to celebrate the power of love.

LOVE IS PASSIONATE

The first two lines of verse 7 mean that it is simply impossible to pour cold water on true love and dissolve it.

Waters and floods are often used in the Bible as a picture of life's hardships. Isaiah 59:19 speaks of the enemy coming in like a flood. Psalm 88:7 says, "Your wrath lies heavy upon me, and you have afflicted me with all your waves."

Affliction is part of life, and part of married life is the fact that the love of a couple is tested—repeatedly—in these waters of affliction and pain. But the amazing thing about love is its survivability. "Suffering and pain, bereavement and loss may test its constancy, but they will not quench it."[1] It is an invincible passion. Sorely tested, it comes through.

Of course, the love of God is just the same. The apostle asks the question in Romans 8:35, "Who shall separate us from the love of Christ? Shall tribulation, or distress, or persecution, or famine, or nakedness, or peril, or sword?" If these various waters of affliction flow over us during our lifetime, will that cut us off from Christ's love? Well, the apostle replies in verses 38 and 39:

> I am persuaded that neither death nor life, nor angels nor principalities nor powers, nor things present nor things to come, nor height nor depth, nor any other created thing [in other words, nothing at all] shall be able to separate us from the love of God which is in Christ Jesus our Lord.

God is so passionate towards his people that he will hold on to them come what may. And, in reflection of that, a husband and wife are glued together in the passion of love through thick and thin. It is part of being made in the image of God.

So we are invited to celebrate the passion of love.

1. Taylor, *Union*, 47.

LOVE IS PRICELESS

The last three lines of verse 8 says that colossal wealth would be utterly despised if a man were to try to exchange it for love. In other words, you just cannot buy love. It is far too valuable for that. If you try, you will make yourself look an utter fool. If a man proposes to a woman, and in the course of his speech says, "I'll make you very rich," but never says, "I love you," she will not be very impressed. You cannot buy love. If a woman abandons her husband, lured by the wealth of a richer man, she becomes despicable.

You cannot buy God's love either. Listen to what Moses said in God's name to the people of Israel in Deuteronomy 7:7–8: "The LORD did not set his love on you nor choose you because you were more in number than any other people, for you were the least of all peoples; but because the LORD loves you." The Lord simply loves. There is absolutely nothing that we can do to secure God's love. He loved his people before we ever existed. The Lord Jesus came into the world because, from eternity God so loved the world.

In the same way, a man cannot swap wealth for love. True love between husband and wife is a priceless gift. It is a reflection of the God in whose image we are made.

So we are invited to celebrate the pricelessness of love.

At this point we must pause to wonder at the love of God which surpasses knowledge, that powerful, passionate, priceless love in Christ crucified for sinners, that love from which nothing can separate us. *That* is a love worth celebrating.

18

Royalty for Everyone

(Song of Solomon 8:8–14)

And so we come, finally, to verses 8–14. They form a sort of appendix, and their theme is that royal love is for everyone.

In the first two verses we hear the voice of a man, followed in verse 10 by that of a woman; then from verses 11 to 13 the man speaks again, and in verse 14 the woman rounds things off.

These are new voices, another man and another woman. No longer are Solomon and Shulamite the speakers. Notice that in verse 11 this man talks about Solomon, and in verse 12 he speaks to Solomon. This is a couple we haven't heard before. Who are they? They represent any man and any woman. The appendix is telling us that what has been described in the relationship between King Solomon and his Shulamite from 1:2 to 8:6 may be the experience of any married couple. The speakers are representative of men and women in general. The joy of marriage which has been described in this royal relationship is for anyone.

The man speaks, then, in verses 8 and 9. He uses the plural of excitement, as he employs the pronoun "we." He is looking forward to his marriage. He is referring to his fiancée when he speaks of "a little sister." We have seen how "sister" in the Song is equivalent to "wife." By speaking of "a little sister," this man means that she is not yet his wife. She is not literally without breasts, but they are not yet available for the man's pleasure. However, the day will come when she will be spoken for, when this engaged couple will be united in marriage, just as Solomon and Shulamite are.

The question at the end of verse 8 is answered by verse 9. What will the husband do? He will regard his new wife as an object of exquisite beauty. Silver and cedar are ornamental. They are decorative. They speak of beauty. Of course this man already knows that his fiancée is beautiful, but when they are married he will appreciate her all the more. In the intimacy of marriage her beauty will be enhanced beyond what is permissible during engagement.

Moreover, the man appreciates that his admiration of his lady's beauty will be redoubled by the confidence that she is a wall against other men, but an open doorway through which he may enter. He is confident that she will preserve her fidelity in marriage.

In verse 10 the woman echoes the same sentiments. She agrees that she is a wall against others. But for her husband to go through the doorway spells peace. So here she is, describing the time when they are married. In verses 8–9 the man says, we're not yet married, but what will it be like when we are! Here the wife responds, saying, this is what it is like, because now we are married at last.

The last line of the verse is a bit ambiguous in the Hebrew. It may mean either that she found peace in him, or that she was a source of peace to him. Very probably the writer intended it to be ambiguous because both are true. He decided, poetically, to economize on words and just use one phrase to say both things. The joy of marriage is peace for both husband and wife in each other's company. In the Bible peace is a larger concept than we think of today. It includes harmony, contentment, satisfaction, joy. All that is in marriage—for anyone.

In verses 11 and 12 the man speaks again. He looks at Solomon, about whom the Song has spoken. Baal Hamon sounds like a place name. However, there is no known place with that name. Probably it is a fictional place name, and its significance is in what it means. Baal Hamon means "lord of great wealth." That is certainly a true description of Solomon if ever there was one. He was a very wealthy king. He had a lavish lifestyle.

But the problem with the lavish lifestyle of the palace was that the vineyard had to be leased to keepers. In the Song, the vineyard refers to the wife in her attractiveness. That very intimate part of the life of the royal couple has been in the care of other people. The keepers may be compared to ladies-in-waiting. They had the responsibility of preparing Shulamite for Solomon's love, for dressing her up in all her finery to be the alluring attraction that Solomon finds her to be.

The thousand silver coins represents great wealth. Isaiah 7:23 uses a similar picture when talking about a coming day of judgement: "It shall happen in that day, that wherever there could be a thousand vines worth a thousand shekels of silver, it will be for briars and thorns." A thousand shekels of silver was a huge income from a vineyard. It represented great wealth. And here is Solomon, the lord of great wealth, finding a wealth of pleasure in his vineyard, his wife. But all the same there were ladies-in-waiting who had to be paid with a few hundred silver coins for their work, as they did their bit to enhance the love life of Solomon and Shulamite.

And now this young man is saying, "Solomon, so what if you have great wealth: you can keep it as far as I'm concerned; my own vineyard is before me. I have no envy of the rich and the famous and the royals." Here is someone who does not have the riches of a Solomon, the millions of pounds (or whatever the equivalent was in those days), but who, nonetheless, enjoys his own love relationship with his own wife, his own precious vineyard.

And this is the real message of the Song of Solomon: this experience of inseparability and joy in married love is not just the privilege of royalty. It is for every man and every woman. Anyone may know the joyful wonder, the intense pleasure, of this gracious gift of a loving God.

How we need to hear this today. So many people seem to think, or seem to have been made to feel, that they have to live up to some ideal that is modeled by the stars—pop stars, film stars, or sports stars—or by the royal family, or by the fashion designers. But the Song of Solomon says, No; just be yourselves, and enjoy yourselves in your own way, because married love is God's gift to everybody.

And this reminds us that the model is not the actresses and the pop stars and the royalty, but God himself. He modeled self-giving love in sending his Son into the world because of the guilt of the world's sin. That is the love which we should seek to reflect in our marriages, when we give ourselves devotedly to each other.

And that is where the Song finishes in the final two verses. This other happy couple are nowhere near as wealthy as Solomon and Shulamite, but they are no less happy. This other couple could be you. Here they invite each other into the playful unity of love.

In verse 13 the husband speaks to the wife, and invites her to speak, because he so loves to hear her voice. "Companions" is an exaggerated way of saying "I"—I'm your companion. He addresses his wife as the one who dwells in the gardens, the garden of love, the place where she is at home, the place where he loves to be with her. He wants to hear her voice. That expression is shorthand for total oneness. The husband is saying, let's be together, let's enjoy each other.

Then in verse 14 the wife responds. She uses the same language that Shulamite used earlier on in chapter 2 verse 17. The word "make haste" is most often used for running away from an enemy. It speaks of desperation. Well, she is saying, let's have the same desperation in our longing for togetherness. Let's run away from the enemy of loneliness. Come and eat the spicy delicacies on the mountains of love.

So the fact is (and this is where the Song leaves us) that you do not have to be royalty to have that ornamented life described in verse 9. The silver and the cedar can be ours, whoever we are. At the wedding of Prince William and Kate Middleton in April, 2011, Richard Chartres, the Bishop of London, said, "In a sense every wedding is a royal wedding with the bride and groom as king and queen of creation." He was right—as Solomon recognized centuries ago: true love will turn every marriage into a royal wedding.

And so these new voices chipping in at the end of the Song of Solomon are telling us that every couple in the world may enjoy the kind of relationship described in this Song. You do not have to be a king. You do not have to be the daughter of a king. Joy in marriage is God's gift to all people. And married love is something worth celebrating.

And as we enjoy marriage, part of God's purpose is that our appetite should be whetted for that day when Christ shall be forever united with his bride, the church. In loving each other within the context of marriage we learn a little more of how Christ loves us, and how we are to love him in response. So let's be celebrating married love, and let's be celebrating our Savior's love.

Bibliography

Alexander, Joseph Addison. *The Psalms Translated and Explained*. Edinburgh: Eliot & Thin, 1864.

Balchin, John A. "The Song of Solomon." In *The New Bible Commentary Revised*, edited by Donald Guthrie and J. Alec Motyer, 579–87. Leicester: Inter-Varsity Press, 1970.

Barnes, Albert. *Notes on the Whole Bible: The Old Testament*. 1847. Kindle Edition.

Bayes, Jonathan F. *Sex, Love, and Marriage—A Celebration: The Song of Solomon*. Eugene: Resources, 2012.

Belcher, Richard P. *The Messiah and the Psalms: Preaching Christ from all the Psalms*. Fearn: Mentor, 2006.

Bloch, Ariel, and Chana Bloch. *The Song of Songs: a New Translation with an Introduction and Commentary*. Berkeley: University of California Press, 1995.

Brooks, Richard S. *A Commentary on the Song of Songs*. Fearn: Christian Focus, 1999.

Bruce, Frederick Fyvie. *1 and 2 Corinthians*. London: Marshall, Morgan & Scott, 1971.

Burrowes, George. *A Commentary upon the Song of Solomon*. 1853. Reprint, London: Banner of Truth, 1958.

Buss, Arnold H. *Psychology: Man in Perspective*. Chichester: Wiley, 1973.

Carr, G. Lloyd. *The Song of Solomon*. Leicester: Inter-Varsity Press, 1984.

Castelow, Ellen. "The Sedan Chair." *The History Magazine*. https://www. historic-uk.com/ CultureUK/Sedan-Chair/

Charles, Elizabeth Rundle. *The Chronicles of the Schönberg-Cotta Family*. 1906. Kindle Edition.

Delitzsch, Franz. *Commentary on the Song of Songs and Ecclesiastes*. Edinburgh: T. & T. Clark, 1891.

Bibliography

Durham, James. *An Exposition of the Song of Solomon*. 1840. Reprint, Edinburgh: Banner of Truth, 1982.

Free Church of Scotland. "John Murray: A Book Review and Some Letters." In *The Monthly Record* (March 1983) 51–53.

Garrett, Duane, "Song of Songs." In *Word Biblical Commentary, Vol. 23B: Song of Songs and Lamentations*, by Duane Garrett and Paul R. House, 3–265. Dallas: Word, 2004.

Gill, John. *An Exposition of the Book of Solomon's Song*. 1854. Carluke: Online Bible Edition, 1987–2016.

Gledhill, Tom. *The Message of the Song of Songs*. Leicester: Inter-Varsity Press, 1994.

Goodspeed, Edgar J. "The Shulammite." *The American Journal of Semitic Languages and Literature* 50 (1934) 102–4.

Hendriksen, William. *The Gospel of Luke*. Edinburgh: Banner of Truth, 1978.

Henry, Matthew. *Commentary on the Whole Bible*. 1710. Carluke: Online Bible Edition, 1987–2016.

Huggett, Joyce. *Two into One: Growing in Christian Marriage*. Leicester: Inter-Varsity Press, 1981.

Mann, William, and James Galway. *Music in Time*. London: Mitchell Beazley, 1982.

Martin, George Currie. *Proverbs, Ecclesiastes, Song of Songs*. The Century Bible 13. Edinburgh: Jack, 1908.

Menuhin, Yehudi, and Curits Wheeler Davis. *The Music of Man*. Toronto: Methuen, 1979.

Olyott, Stuart. *A Life Worth Living and a Lord Worth Loving: Ecclesiastes and Song of Solomon*. Darlington: Evangelical Press, 1983.

Rashi, *Commentary on the Tanach*. CD-Rom: Davka Corporation and Judaica Press, 1998–2008.

Richardson, John P. "Preaching from the Song of Songs? Allegory Revisited." *Churchman* Vol. 108, No. 2 (1994) 135–142.

Still, William. *Song of Solomon*. Aberdeen: Didasko, 1971.

Storms, Sam. *One Thing: Developing a Passion for the Beauty of God*. Fearn: Christian Focus, 2004.

Taylor, J. Hudson. *Union and Communion*. 1894. Reprint, London: Overseas Missionary Fellowship, 1967.

Wikipedia. *Mother Church*. https://en.wikipedia.org/wiki/Mother_church.

Wolf, Herbert. "(Shûshan) Lily." In R. Laird Harris, Gleason L. Archer Jr., and Bruce K. Waltke, eds. *Theological Wordbook of the Old Testament* 2: 914. Chicago: Moody, 1980.